W9-CTQ-114

WORKING WITH

CHILDREN

IN SUNDAY SCHOOL

BY ROBERT FULBRIGHT AND EUGENE CHAMBERLAIN

山河市華人宣道會
SAN JOSE CHINESE ALLIANCE CHURCH
1901 COTTLE AVENUE
SAN JOSE, CA 95125

ED
SU
CH
82

 CONVENTION PRESS
A CHURCH SERVICES AND MATERIALS DIVISION PRODUCT

© Copyright 1974. Convention Press
Church Services and Materials Division
Nashville, Tennessee. All rights reserved
5163–14

EUGENE CHAMBERLAIN, formerly coordinating editor in the Children's Section of the Sunday School Department, is manuscript analyst for the Sunday School Board of the Southern Baptist Convention.

ROBERT G. FULBRIGHT is supervisor of the Children's Section of the Sunday School Department, Sunday School Board of the Southern Baptist Convention.

This book is the text for course 6314 of the subject area 63, Bible Teaching Program, of the Church Study Course.

Dewey Decimal Classification Number: 268.432
Printed in the United States of America

Contents

How to Use
WORKING WITH CHILDREN
IN SUNDAY SCHOOL

WORKING WITH CHILDREN IN THE SUNDAY SCHOOL presents basic information about reaching boys and girls, grades 1–6, and about providing Bible-learning experiences for them through the Sunday School. A quick look at the table of contents gives an overview of the book.

This book is designed as a help for:
- All who work with Children, grades 1–6, in the Sunday School
- Children's Division director
- Church staff members with responsibility for Children's work
- General Sunday School officers
- Denominational workers with responsibility for Children's work
- Others with interest in spiritual growth of boys and girls, grades 1–6

The book may be studied individually or in group study. (For information on requirements for study course credit see "General Requirements for Credit" in back of book.) A resource kit containing a teaching plan and a variety of aids for use in group study is available from Baptist Book Stores.

Chapter 1
Looking at Our Task

Can we talk for a bit, the two of us who are writing this book and you, the reader? If we can develop a mutual understanding of some basic factors in the Christian education of children, what you read in this book will have more meaning. Talking about organizing and equipping departments or about enlisting prospects should be done within a certain framework. May we share with you how we feel and think about basics in the Christian education of children?

I. THE BIBLE SPEAKS TO PERSONS OF ALL AGES

The Bible speaks to persons of all ages. Each receives the Bible's message at his own level. The very young child may be filled with awe and wonder at the birth of a special Baby. The child of early elementary years may be awakened to exciting stories from both the Old and New Testaments. By later elementary years, many children confront the demands of Jesus Christ upon every man and, more especially, on them. With increasing sensitivity, youth deal with the gospel. Throughout adult years, men and women rely upon basic Bible teachings to give direction and meaning to lives which must be worked out under extreme pressures.

The fact that the Bible is written in adult language and that its major concepts are deep and broad is undeniable. Yet who would dare to say that its stories and truths are not intended for boys and girls? The Bible does speak to children.

II. BOYS AND GIRLS NEED BIBLE TEACHING

God intends that boys and girls receive his message. If one is inclined to doubt this statement, let him examine these significant messages from the Old Testament: Deuteronomy 6:4–7; Exodus 12:24–27a; and Exodus 13:3–10.

The Deuteronomy passage comprises of course the verses which are known today as the Shema. The Exodus passages are closely akin to the Shema. Basically, the passages affirm the responsibility of parents and the religious community to share with children treasured truths and practices. Religion, these passages affirm, does not exist in a watertight compartment which should be kept separate from day-to-day living. Rather, the passages assume that adult religious beliefs and practices permeate every moment of adult life. In such a situation, children inevitably want to know why adults think what they think and do what they do.

If for even a fleeting moment one is tempted to feel that the religious education of children is not of supreme importance, let him recall the tenderness with which Jesus received young children. Matthew (Matt. 19:13–15), Mark (Mark 10:13–16), and Luke (Luke 16:15–17) all record what happened when young children were brought to Jesus to be blessed. Jesus' words on the occasion have been favorites of generation after generation: "Suffer little children to come unto me, and forbid them not: for of such is the kingdom of God" (Mark 18:16).

Or note the consideration with which Jesus handled a child in an incident recorded in Mark 9:35–37. The disciples had been arguing among themselves about which of them would be the greatest. Shamefacedly, they kept their silence when Jesus asked them what they had been talking about. It was then that he used a young child as he taught the disciples a lesson.

Even though Jesus used a child to teach the disciples an important lesson, he treated that child as a whole person. Jesus placed the child where all of the disciples could see him, but Jesus did not speak until he had first taken the child in his arms. What assurance that child must have felt knowing that the great Teacher cared for him as a person.

If an individual doubts for a moment that children need sound Bible teaching, let him remember the importance of the elementary school years in the spiritual lives of children. The statistics which Southern Baptists have been accumulating for years say that each year thousands of children between the ages of six and eleven make professions of faith in our churches. When almost any group of adult believers is asked, person after person indicates that he made his decision to follow Jesus during these years. Every new convert needs guidance from more mature Christians as he begins to live the Christian life.

The Old Testament passages to which we referred earlier assumed that children would be repeatedly exposed to the religious practices and beliefs of their elders. Therefore, children would early become seekers after insight into those practices and beliefs. Children would naturally want to know why certain things were said and done. When children asked, "What do those things mean?" parents and others were provided with the teachable moment.

Unfortunately, today too many children grow up without any such demonstration. They come from homes which profess no religious faith. Or they come from nominally Christian homes in which religious practices are so minimal a part of life as to stimulate no questions at all. In such a situation, the church cannot wait for children to ask the key questions. We must actively seek to bring children into teaching-learning situations. It becomes our responsibility to stimulate questions which lead to teachable moments. We must be aggressive in enlisting boys and girls in Sunday School.

III. THE TEACHER IS THE KEY TO LEARNING

Granted that the church has responsibility to teach children God's message, what are some basic aspects of the experience which churches should provide? What matters most in a Sunday School? What must a congregation do to meet its responsibility in Bible teaching? Let's think together for a few minutes about these and some other basic questions. Shall we begin with this question: What is the most important single factor in the teaching-learning situation in which a church shares its faith and concerns with children?

The answer is simple: the teacher or teachers. Every church which is seriously concerned with meeting its responsibility wants of course to provide the very best of equipment. Some churches take almost inordinate pride in providing the latest in projectors, listening centers, teaching machines, magnetic chalkboards, and the like. Nevertheless, the teacher remains the most important factor.

Why should this be so? It is so because teaching a child the truths of the Christian faith is not the same as teaching him basic number facts or geography or music appreciation. Teaching a child the truths of the Christian faith requires a teacher who can share these truths from personal experience. The good Sunday School teacher is not so much a teacher in the usual, secular sense of the word as he is a witness. What does the verse "What time I am afraid, I will trust in thee" (Ps. 56:3) mean to a child whose teacher shares it only as an academic exercise in memorization? If the child is to learn the verse "by heart," he needs a teacher who has truly learned in time of distress and peril to put his faith in God.

"O come, let us worship and bow down: let us kneel before the Lord our maker," says Psalm 95:6. The awe and wonder in these verses is not communicated by dramatic teaching techniques. The spirit of true worship is communicated by the testimony of the teacher who himself truly worships the Lord.

IV. LEARNING IS MORE THAN REPEATING WORDS

In Christian education learning means far more than being able to repeat words. Any child of normal intelligence can learn to repeat John 3:16, even if he does have trouble with *begotten* and *whosoever* and *perish,* even if he has only a foggy notion of what *believe* and *eternal* mean.

Giving the right answer to obvious questions requires no inner experience. The most rudimentary skill in second-guessing, an art in which most children are proficient, lets a child know when his teacher wants a yes. "Is it best to tell the truth at all times?" "Does Jesus love all of us no matter who we are or what we do?" What child wouldn't answer yes unless he just wanted to be aggravating?

Being able to arrange the patriarch's names in proper sequence is of course more than a parlor game. But this skill is not equivalent to grasping the wonder of God's working out his plan to bring a Savior into the world "in the fulness of time."

True religious learning involves the inner life. This kind of learning affects more than the mind. It brings into play the very spirit of the learner. Other forms of learning may effect change at many levels, but the kind of learning which we seek to achieve in the Sunday School setting pierces deep. It results in the dawning of insights, not only about the relationship of men and God or the nature of God, but about one's own highly personal relationship to God.

The achievement of these insights is not the work of the teacher alone. Indeed, this achievement may be viewed as not being the work of the teacher at all. It is in fact the work of the Holy Spirit. "The Comforter, which is the Holy Ghost, whom the Father will send in my name, he shall teach you all things, and bring all things to your remembrance, whatsoever I have said unto you" (John 14:26).

V. TELLING ISN'T ALL THERE IS TO TEACHING

When we talked about the centrality of the teacher in the teaching-learning experience, we emphasized the fact that the teacher testifies to his own experience in living the Christian life. This fact might leave the impression that the teacher only has to tell what his religious faith means to him. Such is not the case.

Actually, the teacher of children must be ready to use every sound teaching technique he can discover. The good teacher examines the techniques used by all others who seek to guide the learning experiences of children. We in Christian education often lean heavily upon what secular educators and psychologists have discovered about how children learn. Relying upon the Holy Spirit to work within the learner, we respect basic laws of learning in our effort to provide the best of conditions under which the Spirit may work.

One thing which every careful student of learning has faced is that people do not learn merely by being told. Even factual information is poorly communicated to a child who is told, in effect, only to sit still and listen. The learner must somehow become more deeply involved with the subject matter. To be truly effective this involvement requires the use of as many senses as possible: hearing, seeing, touching, even smelling and tasting, if possible. To use his senses effectively, the child needs to use the learning skills which he has or is acquiring: reading, writing, numbering, drawing, painting, crafting models and puppets, and map making, for instance. To reach the deepest inner levels of the learner, involvement must touch the learner's emotions. He must, in as far as his experience and skill will let him, get inside the skins of the people about whom he studies. Many forms of drama provide the means.

The teaching methods suggested in Southern Baptist periodicals are built upon these basic truths about learning. These suggestions are more than an effort to copy secular education or to make the learning process fun—though there is a lot to be said for that too. These suggestions are our effort to use every resource at our command to create a situation in which the Holy Spirit may effectively communicate to children the Bible truths which they need to experience.

As you study this book, you will explore many aspects of working with children in Sunday School—rooms and equipment, organization, weekday responsibilities and opportunities of teachers, for instance. As you study each chapter, you will realize that the ultimate purpose of every suggestion is the same: the creation of the best possible learning situation. And the best possible learning situation is that situation in which the Holy Spirit can best do his work.

VI. THE CHALLENGE DEMANDS THE BEST

Everyone with anything to sell claims that his product is the best. Every organization with a program to promote declares that no other organization in all the world works for ends quite so significant as its ends. And most of us listen and discount a large percent of what we hear. We learn to ho hum in order to protect our minds and emotions, knowing that we can't buy everything and devote ourselves to every cause.

But the religious instruction of children, that is the guiding of their experiences in and with the Christian faith and its basic teachings, is truly the cause which demands the best. When we speak of the best, we mean primarily the best of teachers. The best of teachers are not necessarily those of the greatest education, most physical charm, or those with the greatest personal magnetism. But teachers of children must be people with genuine Christian experience and equally genuine concern for sharing that experience with boys and girls.

The demand for the best speaks to the willingness of churches to provide the best physical facilities possible. Good teaching which is achieved under adverse conditions can become even more effective when these conditions are improved.

The demand for the best requires the investment of time and effort. The Christian education of children is not something which we accomplish effortlessly and on the fringes of our time.

The rest of this book will help you to explore the demand for the best.

Chapter 2
Organizing to Reach and Teach Children

Let all things be done decently and in order (1 Cor. 14:40). This admonition from the Bible certainly applies to the tasks of reaching boys and girls and of teaching them the Bible. Unless there is a systematic and organized approach to the unreached, we will not be able to enroll children in Sunday School. Good department organization precedes good Bible teaching.

The total Sunday School is organized into four age divisions: Preschool, Children, Youth, and Adult. All boys and girls in grades one through six, or six through eleven years of age, are in the Children's Division. Within this division, a church will have one or more departments.

I. DETERMINING THE DEPARTMENTS NEEDED WITHIN THE CHILDREN'S DIVISION

Several factors influence the number of Children's departments a church should have. The more obvious factors are: number of children enrolled, number of prospects, department room or space available, leaders available, and equipment needed.

Each year prior to Promotion Day, a careful study should be made to determine the number of Children's departments needed for the coming year. Let's examine how such a study can be made.

1. List the pupil enrollment by grades (or ages).
2. List the prospects by grades (or ages).
3. Total the members and prospects by grades (or ages).
4. Group in departments, not exceeding a total potential enrollment of twenty-six children in any one grouping. Usually it is best when organizing a new department to begin with an enrollment of ten to twelve boys and girls. There should be one worker for approximately each seven children enrolled in the department.

Here is an example from the Calvary Baptist Church.

In using the guidelines, the Calvary Baptist Church determined a need for four Children's departments within the Children's Division. The departments are:

Grades	Pupil Enrollment	Prospects	Workers Needed	Departments Needed
1	8	4	4	1 department with
2	6	5		23 potential pupil enrollment
3	5	7	4	1 department with
4	8	6		26 potential pupil enrollment
5	14	11	4	1 department with 25 potential pupil enrollment
6	10	12	3	1 department with 22 potential pupil enrollment
Totals	51	45	15	

Children's Department A (Grades 1–2)
Children's Department B (Grades 3–4)
Children's Department C (Grade 5)
Children's Department D (Grade 6)

Here is an example from the Poplar Springs Baptist Church.

Grades	Pupil Enrollment	Prospects	Workers Needed	Departments Needed
1	6	4		
2	4	3	4	1 department with
3	5	2		24 potential pupil enrollment
4	4	5		
5	7	2	4	1 department with
6	6	1		25 potential pupil enrollment

By using the guidelines, the Poplar Springs Baptist Church determined a need for two Children's departments within the Division. The departments are:

Children's Department A (Grades 1–3)
Children's Department B (Grades 4–6)

If either of these churches had been interested only in teaching its present pupils and not in reaching others, then a lesser number of departments could have sufficed. However, when churches organize and plan for outreach, boys and girls will be reached for Bible study and eventually for Christ and church membership.

II. SELECTING WORKERS

One cannot overemphasize the importance of good workers in Children's departments. The Bible, the curriculum materials, the equipment, the space—all are utilized at the discretion of the worker. A conscientious teacher with little or no equipment, teaching in crowded conditions, can be instrumental in transforming the lives of children through the biblical message. On the other hand, an unconcerned worker with adequate space, new equipment, and the best curriculum materials can easily be a failure. The difference is in the worker.

What kind of worker should be enlisted to teach children? The following qualifications are suggested as guidelines to consider as workers are enlisted.

1. *One Who Has Experienced the Saving Power of Christ and Is a Loyal Church Member*

Of all the qualifications listed, this one is by far the most important. A Children's worker must have committed his life to Christ and must actively support his church. The first objective in teaching children—that of Christian conversion—requires that all workers have a vital, life-changing experience with Christ.

2. *One Who Loves Children and Is Concerned for the Total Child*

Some adults possess a unique love for children. They understand and sense the various needs of children. These same adults can accept children for what they are and not expect adult behavior from them. Some adults possess the kind of patience that enables them to communicate well with children. They are able to look beyond the child of today and see the potential of later years.

Equally important as loving a child is being concerned about that total child. A teacher cannot isolate the spiritual needs of the child and teach only to meet those needs. A teacher must accept the total child with all of his needs and seek to minister to the total person. This means becoming involved with the child and knowing his spiritual condition. It also means being concerned enough to do something for the child who is hungry or who does not have adequate clothing. During Jesus' earthly ministry, he demonstrated through many actions his concern for the total person.

3. *One Who Continues to Grow Through Bible Study and Prayer*

A worker with children needs to be constantly in tune with God through regular Bible study and prayer. A systematic plan of Bible study will aid his spiritual growth. In addition to studying the Bible as it relates to curriculum materials, a worker will be involved in deep Bible study—studying the Bible book by book or by major themes, for instance.

4. *One Who Is Willing to Study*

In every worker there should be a strong desire to sharpen his skills as a teacher. His efforts to improve will include careful study of the curriculum materials; learning the age-group characteristics and needs; exploring how a child learns; participating in church and associational training activities; and attending state and Convention-wide conference centers.

Studying is a continual process. One never reaches the point where studying is no longer required. The person who seriously studies and seeks to improve his skills is also open to new and better approaches in working with children. The worker who continues-to study and grow does not find change as difficult as the adult who has stopped growing.

5. *One Who Has a Conviction That God Wants Him to Teach*

One should teach children because of a personal conviction that God wants him to teach. God calls different people to do different tasks. He calls some as teachers of children. He may have used a division director or a department director to enlist you, or it may have been a member of the nominating committee he used. With your conviction that God wants you to teach and your commitment to study and grow as a Christian, the Holy Spirit can accomplish great things through you as a Children's Sunday School worker.

6. *One Who Will Visit Children*

Working with children cannot be confined to Sunday morning alone. A worker must be willing to visit enrolled boys and girls as well as the prospects. An alert worker visiting in a home will learn a great deal more about a child than he will merely by observing the child on Sunday morning. A visit also suggests to a child that the worker is truly interested in him as a person. Sunday morning teaching can be extended into homes as workers visit and interpret Sunday School work and materials to parents.

7. *One Who Attends the Weekly Workers' Meetings*

A worker in a Children's department is on a team. Each team member must know how the other team members are going to function if maximum results are achieved. Cooperative teaching or team teaching requires planning by all members of the team. For this reason, planning with other workers in the department is mandatory. (See Ch. 4.)

8. *One Who Is Enthusiastic*

Enthusiasm is the spice of life. It gives any task added sparkle. Christians have more to be enthusiastic about than does anyone else. Children naturally gravitate toward enthusiastic people. The joy of helping children grow and develop toward their God-given potential causes one to be enthusiastic.

9. *One Who Is Neat in Appearance*

When a group of children were asked what they liked most in a teacher, several responded that they wanted teachers who were neat in appearance. It is not necessary for one to dress in expensive clothes to be neat. Neatness and cleanliness add to the attractiveness of workers. Children do notice and are drawn to people who are neat and well groomed.

10. *One Who Is Kind and Considerate*

Kindness and consideration were virtues possessed by Jesus. Jesus can be reflected in our lives when we are kind and considerate. These traits enable one to affirm the worth of other individuals. When he is the object of consideration from the teacher, a child feels he is important. The child also has a model for desirable behavior patterns.

III. ENLISTING WORKERS

After careful consideration has been given to the quality of workers needed with children, how does one go about enlisting these workers?

Many churches find the church-elected nominating committee the most appropriate means for selecting Sunday School workers. Ideally, this committee serves throughout the year and services not only Sunday School, but all church program organizations. This committee is responsible for clearing all prospective workers. After a person has been approved, a member of the nominating committee, the Children's Division director, or a Children's department director will contact the individual about the leadership position. Although many churches prefer an annual election of officers, workers may be elected for a longer term of service with an annual review of their work.

Some churches may not have the potential leadership they need; they must do the best they can with what is available. Standards of leadership must be carefully considered when the potential is small. Each church must face the question of whether to provide the ideal number of workers even though some of them do not have the minimum qualifications or to try to get by with fewer workers, knowing that some will be overloaded.

When a church experiences difficulty in finding adequate numbers of workers, where does it look? Following are some sources to consult:

- Leader training director of the Training Union
- Teachers of Adult classes
- New member orientation group (If your church does not have this group, scan a list of new church members.)
- Church roll
- Talent surveys
- Public school personnel (elementary) within the membership of the church

At the beginning of a church year, it is usually better to elect all of the department directors first (and division directors where they are needed). The directors, in turn, will be involved in contacting and enlisting the workers in their respective departments.

Each prospective worker should be contacted personally. Seldom should the approach be made by mail or phone. A personal contact, pointing out why this person was considered for the position, what is involved in the work, and what would be expected of him if he accepts is invaluable in securing a commitment. A prayer with the prospective worker and the promise to continue to pray with him until his decision is made are also very helpful. Usually he should not be pressed for a decision until he has given thought and additional prayer to the matter.

IV. DESIGNATING THE WORKERS' RESPONSIBILITIES

The workers needed within a department in the Children's Division are:

> department director
> outreach leader
> teacher(s)
> secretary (optional)

In a church that has four or more Children's departments, a division director may be needed. The following sections deal with the duties of each of the department workers and also of the division director.

1. *The Division Director*

The division director serves on the Sunday School council and represents the needs and work of the Children's Division to the council. He also interprets the work of the division as this work relates to overall Sunday School work. The division director should be an experienced Children's worker, have a thorough knowledge of the Children's Division materials, and be able to interpret adequately the objectives and work of the division. He is responsible to the Sunday School director for coordinating Children's Sunday School work.

His duties are to:

(1) Determine the number of Children's departments needed to service the enrollment and prospects.

(2) Enlist department directors in cooperation with the Sunday School director and/or church nominating committee.

(3) Assist department directors in enlisting department workers who have been approved by the Sunday School director and/or church nominating committee.

(4) Work with the department directors in providing and conducting specialized training activities for Children's department workers.

(5) Guide department directors in directing the work in the departments.

(6) Encourage the department directors to use the "Children's Department Sunday School Achievement Guide" as a tool for effectively planning and evaluating their work.

(7) Encourage and coordinate outreach activities within the division.

(8) Coordinate the purchasing of church literature and supplies needed within the division.

(9) Cooperate with Children's workers from other church program organizations in coordinating and planning a well-balanced program of Christian education for children, grades one through six or ages six through eleven.

2. *The Department Director*

The department director assumes both administrative and teaching responsibilities in the department. He is responsible to the Sunday School director (or to the division director if there is one) for planning, conducting, and evaluating the work of the department. In teaching, the director assumes the role of lead teacher, being responsible each Sunday for large group.

His specific duties are to:

(1) Discover, recommend, and enlist workers for the department.

(2) Secure literature and other resources needed for use

in the department, if designated to do so by director.

(3) Lead the workers to make the best use of curriculum materials and other resources.

(4) Enlist workers and guide them in weekly planning for the ongoing work of the department.

(5) Represent the departments on the Sunday School council or to the division director (if there is one.)

(6) Give general direction to the Sunday sessions of the department.

(7) Guide large-group learning activities.

(8) Guide pupils in spiritual growth, including conversion as the Holy Spirit directs.

(9) Involve department workers in the cultivation of members and their families.

(10) Lead the department workers in discovering prospects for the department, cooperating with all prospect-discovery projects and activities conducted by the Sunday School.

(11) Encourage the outreach leader to involve all department workers in discovering and enrolling prospects for the department. This responsibility includes maintaining an up-to-date prospect file for the department.

(12) Make requests for and use appropriately the money, equipment, and space designated for the department in accordance with church policy.

(13) Secure and maintain weekly records and reports on department workers and children. (The director may assign this responsibility to the outreach leader or to the secretary, an optional officer).

(14) Guide the workers in using and maintaining department supplies and equipment.

(15) Maintain up-to-date information and evaluate periodically the department's progress as measured by the "Children's Department Sunday School Achievement Guide."

(16) Determine activities and study which will improve

the skills of the workers in the department.

(17) Regularly evaluate worker and pupil needs, growth, and development in light of the department's responsibilities in these areas.

3. *The Outreach Leader*

The outreach leader is responsible to the department director for planning, conducting, and evaluating the outreach activities of the department. One of the basic outreach responsibilities is to enroll children in Sunday School. For older children outreach also means reaching boys and girls for Christ and for church membership as well as for teaching. In some departments, the outreach leader may also serve as a teacher or a substitute teacher.

His specific duties are to:

(1) Assist the department director in the total work of the department. Coordinate department outreach plans with those of the outreach director of the Sunday School.

(2) Lead the department workers in discovering prospects for the department.

(3) Encourage the department workers to cooperate in all prospect-discovery projects and activities conducted by the Sunday School.

(4) Participate in weekly workers' meeting held for the department.

(5) Involve department workers in the cultivation of prospects and their families, maintain an up-to-date prospect file, and make assignments to workers.

(6) Engage in activities and study which will improve effectiveness in all areas of work.

(7) Serve as a teacher (younger and middle children) or as a substitute teacher (older children).

(8) Guide pupils in spiritual growth, including conversion as the Holy Spirit directs.

(9) Help the department director with records if requested.

4. *The Teacher(s)*

The teacher is responsible to the department director for teaching a group of children. In Bible Learners departments and Bible Discoverers departments, these teaching groups are temporary and will vary from unit to unit. In Bible Searchers departments with permanent groupings, the small group will remain the same throughout the year.

Each teacher is also assigned a permanent group of children for the purpose of home visitation and ministry to the child and his family in Bible Learners and Bible Discoverers departments. In Bible Searchers departments the teaching group and the home-visitation group are the same.

The teacher's specific duties are to:

(1) Guide a small group in the planning and developing of a Bible-learning project during each unit of study. Assist individual learning activities as needed.

(2) Assist the director in large-group learning activities as appropriate.

(3) Cooperate with the department director or outreach leader in discovering and cultivating prospects and their families.

(4) Participate in the weekly workers' meeting held for the department.

(5) Through regular visitation, cultivate the members and their families assigned to his group.

(6) Engage in activities and study which improve his effectiveness.

(7) Guide pupils in spiritual growth, including conversion as the Holy Spirit directs.

(8) Assist the department director in planning, performing, and evaluating the work of the department through use of the "Children's Department Sunday School Achievement Guide."

5. *The Secretary*

A secretary may be added to the department workers when the department director feels the need for such a worker and when a qualified person is available. The secretary is responsible to the department director for handling all matters related to department records and for cultivating assigned pupils and their families. (When a secretary is not used, these duties may be performed by an outreach leader or a teacher.)

His specific duties are to:

(1) Secure and maintain weekly records and reports on department workers' outreach activities, teaching activities, and involvement in performing church functions.

(2) Use records in helping the department director in evaluating the work of the department.

(3) Secure literature and other resources needed for use in the work of the department.

(4) Assist the department director in planning, performing, and evaluating the work of the department. (For instance: Guide a small group in absence or tardiness of a teacher and assist in large-group activities as appropriate.)

(5) Guide pupils in spiritual growth, including conversion as the Holy Spirit directs.

(6) Cooperate with the department director or outreach leader in discovering and cultivating prospects and their families.

(7) Cooperate with the department director in cultivating members and their families.

(8) Engage in activities and study which improve his effectiveness.

V. PREPARING FOR OUTREACH

In the Great Commission, given to his followers just prior to his ascension, Jesus said, "Go . . . teach." (Matt. 28:19–20). Earlier in Jesus' ministry, he said, "Suffer the little children to come unto me, and forbid them not: for of such is the kingdom of God" (Mark 10:14). The instructions are clear: children are important and children need to be taught about God.

Before teaching can occur in Sunday School, the boys and girls must be enrolled. For the Sunday School worker, reaching children for Sunday School enrolment is half of his job.

As a department begins to organize for outreach, consider showing the filmstrip *Outreach for Unenrolled Children* (available from Baptist Book Stores). Then, one of the first steps is to elect an outreach leader for the department. (In smaller departments with only two workers, this responsibility may be assigned to one of the workers.) However, outreach must become the concern of each worker in the department. As the department director enlists workers for the department, the outreach responsibility needs to be clearly identified.

The following steps should be taken as a department seriously considers its outreach responsibilities.

1. *Assign Each Enrolled Child to a Department Worker for Regular Visitation and Home Ministry.*

Each worker should visit his group of children at least once a quarter. Just prior to the beginning of the quarter is a good time to visit and take the literature into the homes. Calling attention to various sections of the pupil's quarterly will entice a child to read and use the material. Home information may be gleaned and recorded in *Children's Sunday School Group Record Book.* Reporting to the parents on progress the child is making and his involvement in the Bible-learning projects will convey to the parents the importance of Bible teaching for children.

Such home visits also offer excellent opportunities to witness to lost parents or to give encouragement to parents who appear to be indifferent toward Christ and the church.

2. *Plan Prospect Discovery Projects for the Department.*

Discovering unenrolled boys and girls is the job of every worker in the department. For suggestion, read *Outreach for Children* by Muriel F. Blackwell (available from Baptist Book Stores). More than fifty different approaches to discovering and cultivating prospects are suggested in this book.

From time to time, churchwide prospect-discovery projects—

such as a census—will be conducted. Encourage all the department workers to participate in these churchwide efforts.

The alert worker will be on constant lookout for unenrolled children. Survey the neighborhood in which you live. A friend who teaches in a nearby elementary school may supply names and addresses of children. A moving van arriving in the community may signal the coming of new prospects. Prospect discovery is a continual process. Names of children should be added to the prospect file each month throughout the year.

3. *Establish and Maintain an Active Prospect File for the Department.*

As prospects are discovered, add their names, addresses, and other vital information to the department prospect file. When children move out of the community, names should be deleted. If information about any prospect changes, the file should be corrected.

The outreach leader maintains an up-to-date prospect file throughout the year. No department is likely to be successful in outreach without a good prospect file.

4. *Assign Each Prospect to a Worker to Visit and Cultivate.*

In addition to his regular group (members), each Sunday School worker will be assigned by the outreach leader one or more prospects to visit and cultivate.

Visiting prospects for the Sunday School means more than just extending an invitation to attend Sunday School. It means sharing with the child excitement about Bible learning that takes place in Sunday School. Taking a pupil's quarterly and leaving it in the home is a reminder to the family of your visit and interest. Establishing rapport with the family will open the door to good communication and witnessing. After friendship has been established, regular visits can be supplemented by telephone calls and personally written notes.

As a worker visits a prospect, he should secure information on other unreached family members. He can then share this information with the Sunday School outreach leader or Sunday School director.

5. *Report on Home Visits at Weekly Workers' Meeting.*

At the weekly workers' meeting, the outreach leader will call for reports on home visits and contacts with both members and prospects. Information gleaned from the contacts can be shared at this time. Special needs can receive prayerful support. As children are enrolled, they are removed from the prospect file and added to the members roll. (See Ch. 4.)

To supplement home visits, send each week a copy of *More* (to first and second graders) or *Adventure* (to third, fourth, fifth, and sixth graders) to absentees and prospects. Either of these leisure-reading papers will say to a home that you are interested in the child. Envelopes may be addressed during the weekly workers' meeting and mailed immediately following. Mailing a leisure-reading paper does not of course take the place of home visits.

6. *Follow Consistent Enrollment Procedures.*

Sunday Schools have followed different enrollment practices through the years. Securing adequate enrollment information is necessary to conduct any outreach projects. It is also important in measuring the success of your outreach efforts. A good enrollment practice is to enrol each prospect the first Sunday he is present in Sunday School. Immediately after the child is enrolled, his home should be visited by a Children's worker. Leaving the leaflet "Your Child and the Sunday School" (available from Materials Services Department, 127 Ninth Avenue, North, Nashville, Tennessee 37234) will help interpret to the parents the objectives of Bible teaching in the Sunday School.

A child's name should be dropped from the Sunday School roll only when:

(1) The child has moved from the community
(2) The child has joined another Sunday School
(3) The child and/or his family requests the name be removed
(4) or in the event of the death of the child.

When outreach is taken seriously by all the workers in the department, unenrolled children will be reached. As departments grow and reach an enrollment of twenty-six pupils, plan to create new departments. New departments will mean that more children can be reached for Bible teaching and eventually for Christ and church membership.

VI. UTILIZING RECORDS

Records carefully taken and properly utilized can greatly assist workers in measuring growth and effectiveness within a Children's department.

A secretary's table placed near the entrance of the department room allows pupils to leave their offering envelopes and reports prior to becoming involved in the small-group learning. The secretary or outreach leader can then compile the records for the department without distracting the teacher from his responsibility of teaching. Each Sunday after the department records are compiled, they are turned in to the general secretary.

Carefully maintaining good records helps workers to keep in touch with the children, to follow up on absentees, and also to plan effectively.

There are two record systems available from Baptist Book Stores from which churches may choose. One is the Six Point Record System, and the other one is the Broadman Record System.

The Six Point Record System includes six points upon which all teachers in Children's departments and all boys and girls in Bible Searchers departments are checked. Bible Learners and Bible Discoverers are checked only on attendance. The points are:

Attendance	20%	Offering	10%
On Time	10%	Prepared Lesson	30%
Bible Brought	10%	Preaching Attendance	20%

The Revised Broadman Record System includes six points with no assigned percentage values. The teachers in all Children's departments and the boys and girls in Bible Searchers departments are checked on each of the points. Bible Learners and Bible Discoverers are checked only on attendance. The points are:

Present	Lesson Studied
Bible Brought	Giving
Bible Read Daily	Worship Attendance

In this system, the member's report also includes a place to indicate the number and kinds of contacts made to prospects and absentees.

The department secretary or outreach leader should secure the necessary forms and take the initiative in helping workers use them, in line with the policy of the church. Basic forms include classification slips, enrollment cards, department record cards, drop and transfer slips, individual record cards for teachers and children, and teacher's record books. All of these forms are available in both record systems. Consult the Baptist Book Store catalogue for form numbers and descriptions.

VII. FOR TEACHING AND OUTREACH

One of the major responsibilities of the department director is to help his workers train themselves for their work. One of the duties of every worker is to improve his skills. Each department worker needs to study the three basic books related to Children's Sunday School work. These books are:

- *Working with Children in Sunday School* (this book)
- *Guiding Children,* Margaret Sharp and Elsie Rives
- *Understanding Children,* Marjorie Stith

Each of these books is a part of the Church Study Course. They are all designed for either individual or group study. Teacher's guides are available for *Guiding Children* and *Understanding Children.* A special Resource Kit is available for *Working with Children in Sunday School,* and this Kit contains both suggestions and aids for teaching the book. With this kind of help a department director may, if necessary, teach these books to his workers. Frequently churchwide or associational study groups will make it possible for workers to study under the guidance of other qualified Children's workers.

In addition to the study of the three basic books, the weekly workers' meeting offers another in-service training opportunity. You will find further discussion of the weekly workers' meeting in Chapter 4.

Each year special conferences for Children's Sunday School workers are held at the Ridgecrest and Glorieta Conference Centers. A wise department director will encourage workers to attend these conferences as well as meetings sponsored by his state Sunday School department.

VIII. SUMMARY AND REVIEW

Take a moment to consider what you have discovered as you have read this chapter. Answering the following questions will help you analyze what you have learned. If you have difficulty with any questions, scan again the part of the chapter with which that question deals.

● How can one determine how many departments are needed in the Children's Division in the Sunday School of his church?

● Name at least seven characteristics of a good Children's Sunday School worker.

● Does your Sunday School department have the workers it needs to do the best job of reaching and teaching boys and girls? If not, what additional workers are needed?

● In the light of the suggestions in the chapter, evaluate the way in which you were enlisted as a Children's Sunday School worker.

● List your own duties as a Sunday School worker and compare that list with the list for your position as given in this chapter.

● What are the major steps a Children's Sunday School department must take in preparing for outreach?

● How can your department improve in its use of records as a resource for better reaching and teaching boys and girls?

● Name the three basic books which every worker with Children in Sunday School should study.

Chapter 3
Considering the Children

The years from grade one to grade six bring dramatic changes in boys and girls. Sizes change. New skills are developed. Changed attitudes come into play. Compared to himself at age six, nearly any eleven-year-old seems an almost altogether different creature. For this reason children in the Children's Division are best understood when the age span is broken into smaller segments: Bible Learners, Bible Discoverers, and Bible Searchers. Boys and girls at these different levels have special characteristics. Some approaches useful at one level are relatively ineffective at another.

The purpose of this chapter is to help you explore in more detail the distinctives of the grades or ages in which you are most interested. Even though you are primarily concerned with only one of the groups, you will likely enjoy and profit from reading about the others.

For your convenience the chapter is divided into Sections A, B, and C. Section A deals with Bible Learners, primarily boys and girls in first and second grades. Section B deals with Bible Discoverers, primarily boys and girls in third and fourth grades; and Section C deals with Bible Searchers, primarily boys and girls in fifth and sixth grade.

Section A begins on page 35 . Section B begins on page 55, and Section C begins on page 75. Select the section in which you are interested and turn directly to it now.

Learning

I am six—reaching-for-seven;
Thrust headlong into the world of learning;
My inquisitive mind a kaleidoscope of why's,
Launching me on a lifetime quest.

And you teach
Indelibly with word and deed,
Intriguing me with words,
Challenging me with example.

I am six—reaching-for-seven,
Then I'm gone beyond this six-seven world,
This kaleidoscope. Together let's focus the why's
into lovely patterns.

—Muriel F. Blackwell

SECTION A
BIBLE LEARNERS

Entering the formal world of learning, six- and seven-year-olds bring an array of experiences to Bible-teaching situations at church. Compared with boys and girls a generation or two back, these children use larger vocabularies. They have eye-witnessed global events via television. However, the same medium which tends to increase vocabularies and broaden learning experiences may also introduce children to violence and crime unknown to many adults two generations back.

The surge of a technetronic age, the mobility of a society forcing parents to be uprooted, and the instability of home life all create frustrations and problems for the child. Nevertheless the advance in science and automation and the hurry-up pace of our society have not changed the pacing of the child's own physical, emotional, mental, and spiritual development.

Who are the children we are referring to as Bible Learners? In many churches this group will be made up of first and/or second graders (six and/or seven year olds). In churches where there are few children, the Bible Learners group may be composed of first, second, and third graders (six-, seven-, and eight-year-olds).

First-grade department   Second-grade department First- and second-grade department First-, second-, and third-grade department

See Chapter 2 for detailed suggestions on how to organize your Bible Learners department.

Bible Learners form the first grouping in the Children's Division. Having been promoted from the Preschool Division (five-year-old department), children are learning to go from *equipment-structured activities* (such as blocks, home-living, and puzzles) in Preschool to *content-structured activities,* referred to as Bible-learning projects, in the Children's Division. For the first time, boys and girls are involved with teachers in planning units of study. Pupils select Bible-learning projects that help achieve learning goals within the unit. They begin to learn to use the basic learning skills they are acquiring—reading and writing.

Even though a child in a Bible Learners department is now in school, his learning skills are very limited. The first grader is learning to read and write and live within some well-defined boundaries. Expecting him to utilize refined learning skills at this age only adds to his frustration.

The alert teacher will look for ways to reinforce a child's reading and writing skills. For example, Bible verses for the department will be written in manuscript; color and number coding will be employed to aid the child in learning games and activities. When reading to the child, workers will carefully pronounce words. Pictures will be used to identify new words and to introduce biblical characters and concepts. Great care should be taken to help the child achieve and to feel a sense of accomplishment and satisfaction. Children will not be expected to read difficult Bible verses.

Because the child of this age has entered the formal world of books, churches are encouraged to present a Bible to each child entering the Children's Division. This presentation is usually made on Promotion Day as the child leaves the Preschool Division and enters the Bible Learners Department in the Children's Division. A Bible with special helps for the beginning user is available from Baptist Book Stores. It is the Broadman Presentation Bible. More will be said later in the section about the child and his Bible.

I. A LOOK AT BIBLE LEARNERS

Good Sunday School teaching must begin where the learner is. The teaching must be challenging enough to capture the learner's interest. As the learner becomes involved, he utilizes his skills and knowledge. Therefore, understanding the children we teach is extremely important. Time has a way of erasing from the memory of adults the trials and perplexities of a six- or seven-year-old child.

Have you observed a teacher who had forgotten that first and second graders are only beginning readers? Or a teacher who forgot that boys and girls of this age cannot sit still for long periods of time? Teachers who overlook the characteristics of children—or what is normal conduct for them at this period in life—will not likely meet children's needs. These teachers often expect the boys and girls to act like miniature adults. Normal behavior patterns of children may be interpreted as "mean" or "bad."

The following pupil characteristics and the resulting learning readinesses dictate to the conscientious teacher the kind of physical space needed, the length of time blocks to be used in the teaching-learning process, the size of groups, the degree of interpersonal relationships that can be achieved, and the methods appropriate for the learner. Therefore understanding the following **characteristic** is extremely important in good Sunday School work with Bible Learners.[1]

1. *Physical*

　(1) He is active, constantly moving some part of his body.

　(2) He likes to handle and investigate objects.

　(3) He is increasingly able to use his small muscles.

　(4) He has attained a moderate level of coordination and motor skills.

　(5) He is eager to make use of his abundant energy and rapidly developing physical skills.

　(6) He is losing his baby teeth and acquiring permanent teeth.

　(7) He needs occasional periods of inactivity but becomes restless if required to sit still for long periods of time.

　(8) His eye muscles are becoming better developed, and he is achieving a better eye-hand coordination.

---

[1] This listing of characteristics is based on similar lists in *The Curriculum Base Design of The Sunday School Board of the Southern Baptist Convention,* Nashville, Tennessee. © Copyright 1974, The Sunday School Board of the Southern Baptist Convention. All rights reserved. Used by permission.

(9) He can care for most of his own bodily needs.

(10) He tires easily, needing a frequent change of pace and sufficient rest.

2. *Intellectual*

(1) He thinks literally in concrete, realistic terms and has great difficulty with abstract and symbolic terms.

(2) He is capable of concentration for short periods of time when interested and challenged.

(3) He can make many types of choices with adequate guidance. (He does need help in following through on activities which require long-term action.)

(4) He is ready to think for himself about things within his own experiences.

(5) He has some ability to express ideas, understand cause and effect, solve problems, reason, and plan.

(6) He is learning to use some basic skills such as reading, writing, and oral communication.

(7) He learns quickly and is capable of memorizing short statements.

(8) He is imaginative and creative.

(9) He enjoys doing his own work but sets high standards for himself. He compares his work with that of others and is capable of some evaluation of what he has done.

(10) He demonstrates great curiosity and a variety of interests.

(11) He is more alert mentally when he has proper rest and nutrition.

(12) He enjoys reading aloud and is interested in learning new words.

(13) He can learn from experiences of others as well as from experiences of his own.

(14) He frequently has difficulty in distinguishing between fact and fiction.

(15) He is basically oriented to the here and now.

(16) He has difficulty in sequencing events in relationship to time and history.

(17) He is interested in current events although he is unable

to relate how the events affect him.

3. *Social*
    (1) He can accept simple rules, organization, responsibility, and leader/follower roles in group activities.
    (2) He enjoys playing simple games, dramatizing, and making believe.
    (3) He has some ability to recognize and appreciate individual differences among persons.
    (4) His social relationships are affected very little by sex differences.
    (5) He has a need for companionship and approval of his peers but has a strong need for adult approval and support.
    (6) He is capable of recognizing and respecting the needs and rights of others but is motivated primarily by self-centered interests.
    (7) He has a hard time being understanding and considerate of others.
    (8) He can cooperate with a group in working toward a common goal.
    (9) He can get along well with others in a group activity but is capable of strong criticism of others.
    (10) He is developing a conscience, value system, behavior patterns, and a personality all his own.
    (11) He normally feels good will toward people of different races and nationalities.

4. *Emotional*
    (1) He is beginning to learn to cope with success and failure.
    (2) He is ready for increasing responsibility and opportunities for self-direction and independent thinking.
    (3) He is able to accept and work toward short-term goals.
    (4) He craves acceptance, encouragement, love, and approval and will go to great lengths to get them.
    (5) He feels deeply about his own experiences but is not always sensitive to the feelings of others.
    (6) He is easily swayed emotionally.

(7) His feelings strongly influence his actions.

(8) His self-concept is developing, but often he is unable to describe his feelings about himself.

(9) He is sensitive to criticism and reacts emotionally when reprimanded severely.

(10) He is capable of experiences that involve feelings, imagination, and thought.

(11) He can identify and cope with some of his emotions.

(12) He is easily moved by the pain and sorrow of someone else.

(13) He resents being talked down to but is frustrated if more is expected of him than he is able to do.

5. *Spiritual*

(1) He can learn accepted limits for behavior in his world.

(2) He is easily influenced as he develops values by which to live.

(3) He is developing a conscience and a value system.

(4) He finds it easy to love and trust God and Jesus unquestioningly and to accept the Bible as a unique book.

(5) He is capable of experiences that involve feelings, imagination, thought, and choice-making.

(6) He is forming concepts of his own personal worth.

(7) He has a growing interest in spiritual matters that affect his life.

(8) He is developing a sense of right and wrong, but his understanding of truthfulness and honesty is still vague.

(9) Many children this age do not realize that their sin and wrongdoing is against God and that they should ask God for forgiveness.

(10) He can pray to God and can believe his prayers are heard and will be answered.

(11) He is capable of putting into practice many Bible teachings.

(12) He thinks of the church building as a special place to learn about God and Jesus.

(13) He is able to take responsibility for his behavior.

(14) He can accept God as Creator and trust in God's love and care. He wants to know more about God and the world.

(15) He can think of Jesus as his best friend and helper.

II. PURPOSEFUL OBJECTIVES IN TEACHING BIBLE LEARNERS — Grades 1-2 (Ages 6 & 7)

In a rapidly changing world, people need some constants. Broad objectives in teaching children are such constants. Methodologies may come and go, but these objectives remain. They represent our long-range targets, the outcomes we hope to accomplish as the child grows, develops, and assimilates Bible truths.

The basic objectives may be grouped under seven major heads. Each heading indicates an area in which growth must come if a person is to achieve true spiritual maturity.

Because of individual differences among children, not all of the goals will be reached during the sixth and seventh years of every child's life. This is why "foundational teaching" becomes so important. Teachers of Bible Learners can lay foundations upon which other teachers may build, thus realizing the fulfillment of some of these objectives later in life.

Because of more rapid development or a greater number of learning experiences, some children may proceed much further than others. We must remember that learning is an individual matter. We do not teach groups of children—we teach individuals. Some children are slower in development than others. They may be known as "late-bloomers." If we try to hurry the developing process, we usually hurt or bruise the one we are trying to help. Therefore, care should be taken to aid each child, realizing his growth rate is all his own and cannot be hurried.

Let us now examine each of seven major objectives with regard to first and second graders:[2]

---

[2] This presentation of objectives is based on information in *The Curriculum Base Design of The Sunday School Board of the Southern Baptist Convention,* Nashville, Tennessee. © Copyright 1974, The Sunday School Board of the Southern Baptist Convention. All rights reserved. Used by permission.

1. *Christian Conversion*

The teaching objective is to lay foundations for a genuine Christian conversion experience on the part of each child when he is ready for it. Ways a Bible Learner can move toward the fulfillment of this objective are to:

- Feel love and reverence for God.
- Know that God loves him.
- Have a real desire to do things that please God.
- Grow in his understanding of ways he can please God.
- Learn to love and trust Jesus as his friend.
- Have a growing awareness that Jesus is God's Son.
- Grow in his understanding of what it means to forgive.
- Know that God wants to forgive him when he does wrong.
- Develop a consciousness of his personal need for God's help in doing right things.
- Feel free to approach Christian adults for understanding guidance.

2. *Church Membership*

The teaching objective is to lay foundations for an understanding of what it means to be a church member following the Christian conversion experience.

3. *Christian Worship*

The teaching objective is to help each child in the developing of his ability to participate actively and intelligently in worship and to find satisfaction in worship experiences.

4. *Christian Knowledge and Understanding*

The teaching objective is to help each child gain knowledge of the Bible and Christian faith which can be related to his daily experiences. The objective is sought with respect to the Bible, the great realities of the Christian faith, the Christian movement, the local church, and the denomination.

5. *Christian Attitudes and Convictions*

The teaching objective is to guide each child in the continuing development of attitudes and appreciations that will encourage personal growth. We seek to help the child develop sound attitudes and appreciations regarding God, the meaning of existence, self, others, the Bible, divine institutions, and the present world.

6. *Christian Living*

The teaching objective is to guide each child to develop and use in everyday life habits and skills which will help him grow spiritually.

7. *Christian Service*

The teaching objective is to guide each child to use his talents and skills in ways that will help others.

III. TOOLS FOR WORKING WITH BIBLE LEARNERS

First and second graders have unique needs; and to meet the needs, special materials are provided exclusively for this group. In this section we will look at the curriculum materials provided by The Sunday School Board of the Southern Baptist Convention, (lesson-course materials), and additional resource materials for workers, and at curriculum-related filmstrips based on Bible stories suitable for this age.

1. *Curriculum Materials*

The lesson course materials cover various parts of the Bible which speak to the experiences of first- and second-grade children. Children of this age have experienced a limited range of emotions and problems. The development of the Bible material is influenced by the level at which children perceive their emotions and problems, by their limited school experiences, by their limited concepts of time and space, and by their pattern of concrete thinking. Yet these children can be introduced to the events of Bible history, to most of the major Bible characters, and to most of the major teachings of the Christian faith on a rudimentary level.

Children of this age can best understand the narrative type of biblical literature. Their understanding of narrative is limited chiefly by their vocabulary, though their life experiences may limit their perception of a narrative's implication. Boys and girls have a limited understanding of the main thrust of poetry and prophecy involving symbolism, and they take most passages literally.

Bible Learners are beginning to have an understanding of the human motives which caused Bible people to behave as they did, and these pupils are beginning to understand the obvious consequences of their own actions. Because children of this age cannot place Bible people and events in chronological order or relationship, units of Bible study built around themes are desirable.

The curriculum materials for Bible Learners are planned new each year. Careful consideration is given to provide balance, comprehensiveness and progression. The basic objectives discussed earlier are foremost in the development of a curriculum plan. Some important factors concerning the curriculum materials are:

- Curriculum materials are Bible based.
- Curriculum materials are oriented to the age of the learner.
- Curriculum materials reflect sound educational principles.
- Curriculum materials are doctrinally sound.
- Curriculum material writers are carefully chosen.

The following periodicals are included in the Bible Learners series:

(1) *Bible Learners*

This periodical is intended for pupils to use at home and at church. Children are encouraged to read the stories and other features as often as they like. Using *Bible Learners* helps a child build a love and appreciation for the Bible.

The quarterly contains a Bible story for each Sunday. It also includes a memory verse for each week. In addition, it suggests things to do at home related to unit purposes. Other features are songs, short stories, and additional resource materials related to the unit purposes.

Every pupil and every worker in the department needs a copy of *Bible Learners*. Enough additional copies should be ordered each quarter to allow for new members, for prospects, and for the loss of some quarterlies.

(2) *Bible Learners: Teacher*

This periodical provides workers with the information they need in order to perform the task of teaching the Bible to boys and girls in their department.

Contents include session-by-session Bible study for the worker with suggested teaching procedures, as well as suggestions specifically related to each unit. Bible-learning projects are included for each unit along with memory verses for each session. There are also articles of a helpful and general nature which the worker may wish to clip and save. Resources such as songs are a part of the periodical.

Each worker in the department needs to receive a copy of *Bible Learners: Teacher* each quarter.

(3) *Teaching Pictures for Bible Learners*

This picture set provides enrichment for teaching-learning experiences in the department, both in the large group and in the small groups. Each quarter the set contains thirteen pictures in full color. Some are photographs and some are paintings. Each picture is approximately twelve by seventeen inches in size and should be retained after the quarter and filed in a department picture file. Additional teaching suggestions are also included on the back of each picture.

A filing subject is assigned to each full-color picture. After each quarter is over, pictures should be filed by subject in a permanent department file. The filing system is described fully in a Program Help entitled *How Do I File My Pictures?*, available from the Materials Services Department of the Sunday School Board.

Each department needs at least one set of teaching pictures each quarter.

(4) *Resource Kit for Bible Learners*

This package of planned enrichment materials may be used in both large-group and small-group teaching. Such items as Bible-learning games, Bible-related puzzles, illustrated Bible verses, recordings, and filmstrips may be included. Items are included that relate to each unit in the quarter.

Each department needs at least one Resource Kit each quarter.

(5) *More*

This weekly paper is designed for the beginning reader to use for leisure reading and to reinforce the Bible story used each Sunday in *Bible Learners*. *More* includes at least one learning game or puzzle each week related to the Sunday morning Bible story as well as wholesome entertainment and character-building emphases not directly related to the curriculum. Use of the paper helps a child to develop a positive attitude toward reading church-related materials.

In addition to a Bible emphasis each week, *More* contains stories about real and fictional people and things, a poem, and suggestions for creative activities. The paper is well illustrated and is in full color.

Each child and each worker present should receive a copy each week. Additional copies should be ordered to mail each prospect.

(6) *Children's Leadership*

This periodical is designed to assist the department director in administering the work of the department, to guide him in developing workers, and to help him interpret the Sunday School program in terms of the department with which he works. It also provides outreach projects with suitable suggestions for the outreach leader to use in implementing these plans. In addition *Children's Leadership* provides help for Children's Division directors, Children's Worship Service leaders, and for church staff members with responsibility for children in Sunday School.

An important part of *Children's Leadership* is the planning section for workers with Bible Learners. Detailed suggestions are given for each unit of study in the quarter. The periodical also carries general articles of interest to all Children's workers.

The department director and the outreach leader should each receive a copy of the magazine each quarter.

2. *Resource Materials*

The following materials are helpful for workers with Bible *Learners*. They are available at the Baptist Book Store.

Blackwell, Muriel, *Outreach for Children*. Nashville, Tennessee: Convention Press, 1971.

Chamberlain, Eugene, *When Can a Child Believe?* Nashville, Tennessee: Broadman Press, 1973.

Fulbright, Robert G., *New Dimensions in Teaching Children*. Nashville, Tennessee: Broadman Press, 1971.

Ingle, Clifford, editor, *Children and Conversion*. Nashville, Tennessee: Broadman Press, 1970.

McElrath, William N., *A Bible Dictionary for Young Readers*. Nashville, Tennessee: Broadman Press, 1965.

McElrath, William N., *Bible Guidebook*. Nashville, Tennessee: Broadman Press, 1972.

Rives, Elsie and Sharp, Margaret, *Guiding Children*. Nashville, Tennessee: Convention Press, 1969.

Songs for Children (formerly *Songs for Primaries*). Nashville, Tennessee: Broadman Press, 1964.

Stith, Marjorie, *Understanding Children*. Nashville, Tennessee: Convention Press, 1969.

3. *Curriculum-related Filmstrips for Use with Children*
   (1) "Children's Resource Filmstrips"
   - *Making Choices*
   - *Church*
       Frames 1–18: What Do Churches Do?
       Frames 19–28: Church Helpers
       Frames 29–40: Learning Church Manners
       Frames 41–50: Worship Service
   - *Bible Background*
       Frames 1–20: The Land of the Bible
       Frames 21–50: What Is the Bible?
   - *Making Friends*
       Frames 1–15: Bible Friends
       Frames 16–26: What Makes a Good Friend
       Frames 27–50: Learning How to Be Friendly
   (2) "Children's Resource Filmstrips II"
   - *The Christian Way*
   - *Who Am I?*
   - *Helpers*
   - *We Learn Together*
   (3) "Getting to Know God Better"
   - *Getting to Know God through Jesus*
   - *Getting to Know God through the Bible*

- *Getting to Know God through Prayer and Worship*
- *Getting to Know God through the World*

(4) *Home and Family Relationships*

(5) *Learning to Be Yourself*

(6) *The Story in the Bible*

(7) *The Land Where Jesus Lived*

(8) "Bible Story Series"

- *Jesus and His Helpers:* "Supper on a Hillside," "Philip the Missionary"
- *When the People Listened:* "Rules for Happy Living," "Ezra Reads the Scroll"
- *Dependable Joseph:* "Joseph and His Family," "Faithful Joseph"
- *God's Plan for Me:* "God's Care for Moses," "How Daniel Grew"

(9) "Bible Story Series II"

- *Jesus and His Life:* "Jesus the Boy," "Jesus the Man"
- *Story the Bible Tells:* "Old Testament," "New Testament"
- *Life of Paul:* "Early Life," "Missionary Journeys"
- *Friends of Jesus:* "Peter," "John," "Mary and Martha," "Lazarus," "Zacchaeus"

4. *Filmstrips for Use in Leadership Training*

(1) *Teaching Bible Learners*

(2) *Outreach for Unenrolled Children*

(3) *Teaching Children the Bible*

(4) *Using Music with Children*

(5) *A Learning Environment for Children*

(6) *Using Creative Dramatics with Children*

(7) *The Preadolescent*

(8) "Teaching Improvement Series: Children"

- *The Adventure of Unit Teaching*
- *These Are Your Children*
- *You—a Worker with Children*
- *Ways to Help Children Learn*

(Note: All of the listed filmstrips are produced by Broadman Films and are available at Baptist Book Stores.)

5. *Program Helps*
    (1) *Guidelines for Bible Study for Workers with Preschoolers and Children*
    (2) *How Do I File My Pictures?*
    (3) *Preschool and Children's Workers Witnessing*
    (4) *Your Child in the Sunday School*

(Note: Program Helps are available from Materials Services Department 127 Ninth Avenue, North, Nashville, Tennessee 37234.)

IV. GROUPING BIBLE LEARNERS WITHIN THE DEPARTMENT

There are two kinds of groupings for Bible Learners. One is for home ministry and visitation, and the second grouping is for teaching in the small group on Sunday morning.

The first grouping for home ministry and visitation should be made at the beginning of the year—or just prior to promotion time. The director or outreach leader will divide the names of the children equally among the workers in the department. Usually the children will be grouped by geographical areas and the names of the children given to a teacher who lives in or near the same vicinity. Each teacher then visits the children in his group on a regular basis. Such visit will include taking the pupil's quarterly to him; calling during sickness, sorrow, or other family crisis and visiting simply to show interest. When a child in his group is absent, the worker will either visit, send a note, or call to express concern and show friendship.

The second grouping is for the small groups that are formed for each unit of study for the purpose of Bible learning. Because learner needs are based on interest and involvement, children are given an opportunity the first Sunday of each unit to choose a Bible-learning project on which to work during the entire unit.

Thus small groups are formed, consisting of two to seven children, and remain together for the unit. When the unit is culminated, these small groups dissolve. Then another new unit is introduced, other Bible-learning projects chosen, and new small groups are formed. Therefore, the grouping for teaching Bible Learners is referred to as a temporary grouping.

Detailed help for introducing the unit of study and forming the temporary groups is given in the curriculum materials on a regular basis.

V. A BIBLE LEARNER AND HIS BIBLE

Children soon sense the importance and value placed on different things by adults. Daily newspapers come into the home, are read, and immediately disposed of. Library books are checked out to a reader, remain in his possession for a short time, and then are returned to the library, never to be read again. Classics are purchased—sometimes read—and placed on a bookshelf.

What message do you convey to the child about the Bible? Is it read regularly? Is it used each Sunday morning in the department? Is great care taken to introduce its important teachings to children? Is it the focal point for teaching in both small and large group?

Several versions of the Bible should be available in a Bible Learners department. A department Bible with large print and pictures is good to use in the large group while telling the Bible story. Opening the Bible while telling the story says to the children that the story is from the Bible. Voice inflections, facial expressions, and mood can convey the importance of this story felt by the storyteller. Underlining verses in the department Bible alerts children to truths in the story.

VI. BIBLE LEARNERS AND MEMORY VERSES

Bible Learners are encouraged to memorize a short Bible verse each Sunday. Bible verses for children this age are carefully selected and printed in both teacher and pupil materials. As children learn these verses, they may sense the importance of God's Word. Bible verses related to children's experiences are the most desirable. The verse, "What time I am afraid, I will trust in thee," (Ps. 56:3) may help a child to be calm in a fear-producing situation. The verse may also help him feel the protective care of God.

A word of caution to the teacher who has children memorize for the sake of memory alone: It is far more important for a child to understand what he has learned and associate that learning with everyday living than merely to be able to quote words in correct order. Drill in memorizing can make this learning experience unpleasant for children. When memory work is used as a basis for conventional teaching, concepts can be transmitted and positive learning can occur.

VII. SUMMARY AND REVIEW

In Section A you have looked at:
- physical, intellectual, social, emotional, and spiritual characteristics of Bible Learners
- objectives in teaching Bible Learners
- tools for working with Bible Learners
- how to group Bible Learners for teaching and reaching
- how to help Bible Learners use the Bible
- how to help Bible Learners with memory verses

Take a moment to reflect on what you have read in light of your experiences in the department in which you teach. Try to spot at least three things you will do as a result of your study of Section A.

Now you are ready to move to Chapter 4. That is, you are ready to move to Chapter 4 unless you want to explore distinctives about teaching and reaching Bible Discoverers or Bible Searchers.

Discovering

I am eight-reaching-for-nine.
Each day brings new discoveries to my world,
Giving me a keener sense of life and living;
My questioning mind enlarging my kaleidoscope of why's.

Eagerly I share your grown-up world,
Trusting your wisdom, trying to match it with my own,
Asking, discovering, and sharing knowledge new to me.

And you teach,
Taking my hand, leading me along the discovery road,
Helping me with this kaleidoscope of why's.

My eight-nine world is but a fleeting moment.
Together let's discover worthwhile paths.
                            —Muriel F. Blackwell

SECTION B
BIBLE DISCOVERERS

The children of third- and fourth-grade level—eight and nine year olds—approach the Bible-teaching situations in Sunday School with an array of backgrounds and experiences. Feeling more secure than first and second graders in Bible study, these boys and girls are experiencing many transitions. They are moving from simple learning situations to more complex learning situations; they are beginning to change from teacher-pleasers to peer-pleasers. In learning skills, the third grader is moving from manuscript printing to cursive writing, from simple math to the multiplication facts.

The rapidly changing society is having its effect on boys and girls. Bombarded by radio and television, the eight- and nine-year-olds are using a larger, more sophisticated, and technical vocabulary than a generation ago. The mobile society has helped sever family ties with grandparents, aunts, and uncles. With one-third of the families in America moving each year, the children are faced with forced adjustments. Difficulty in making these adjustments sometimes shows up in overt behavior problems. The instability of homelife creates frustrations and problems for many children. Yet all the change and advancement in technology has not hurried the pacing of any child's own physical, emotional, mental, and spiritual development.

Let's take a closer look at the group we are referring to as Bible Discoverers. In most churches this group will be made up of third and/or fourth graders (eight- and nine-year-olds). In a few churches where there is a very limited number of children in the entire Children's Division, the group may include children in grades one through six (six through eleven year olds).

Third-grade department   Fourth-grade department
Third- and fourth-grade department
Grades-one-through-six department.

See Chapter 2 for detailed suggestions on how to organize your Bible Discoverers department.

Work done with third and fourth graders is built upon the work done with them in younger departments. Because the boys and girls are developing more learning skills, they can be called upon to do more in the Bible Discoverers department than ever before. They can now take a more active role in unit planning and in identifying and developing Bible-learning projects. Map study and research are two examples of new learning activities in which Bible Discoverers may engage. Even though their ability to sequence events from Bible study is very limited, they are beginning to understand how various parts of the Bible fit together and are beginning to appreciate the relationship of one biblical generation to another. Bible Discoverers are beginning to understand cause and effect and can understand that human actions have consequences.

I. A LOOK AT BIBLE DISCOVERERS

Good Sunday School teaching must begin where the learner is. Only when each child is taken where he is and challenged to progress as far as he can go, will his achievement and the total achievement of the department approach the maximum. Teaching must be challenging enough to capture the child's interest. As the learner becomes involved, he utilizes his skills and knowledge. Therefore, understanding the children we teach is extremely important.

Time has a way of erasing from the memory of adults the trials and perplexities of third and fourth graders. Have you observed a teacher who had forgotten that third and fourth graders have only limited learning skills? Have you noticed that third and fourth graders forget easily and have to be reminded often? Or have you observed a teacher who forgot that boys and girls of this age cannot sit still for long periods of time? Teachers who overlook the characteristics of children—or what is normal conduct for them at this period in life—will not likely meet children's needs. These teachers often expect the boys and girls to act like miniature adults. Normal behavior patterns of children may be interpreted as "mean" or "bad."

These pupil characteristics and the resulting learning readiness dictate to the conscientious teacher the kind of physical space needed, the length of time blocks to be used in the teaching-learning process, the size of groups, the degree of interpersonal relationships that can be achieved, and the methods appropriate for the learner.

Therefore, understanding the following characteristics is extremely important in good Sunday School work with Bible Discoverers.[3]

1. *Physical*
   (1) He is increasingly able to use his small muscles.
   (2) He is attaining a good level of general coordination and use of motor skills.
   (3) He is eager to make use of his abundant energy and rapidly developing physical abilities.
   (4) He tends to overdo and needs periods of relaxation and quiet after strenuous activity.
   (5) Girls are maturing more rapidly than boys.
   (6) He can make full use of his eyes since eye-muscle development is nearing completion.
   (7) He can care for his own bodily needs.
   (8) He is very active, constantly moving some part of his body.

---

[3] This listing of characteristics is based on similar lists in *The Curriculum Base Design of The Sunday School Board of the Southern Baptist Convention*, Nashville, Tennessee. © Copyright 1974, The Sunday School Board of the Southern Baptist Convention. All rights reserved. Used by permission.

2. *Intellectual*
   (1) He can make many types of choices but may not follow through on those which require long-term action.
   (2) He is beginning to think for himself, form opinions, and recognize that his parents and teachers can make mistakes.
   (3) He has limited ability to generalize or understand cause and effect, but he is able to express his ideas, solve problems, reason, and plan.
   (4) He thinks literally and is realistic.
   (5) He is capable of concentration when interested and challenged.
   (6) He enjoys reading, research, fact finding, map study, and writing unless he is expected to work at too great a level of difficulty.
   (7) He can employ imagination and creativity.
   (8) He demonstrates great curiosity and a wide variety of interests.
   (9) He needs clues in order to do quick recall, and he remembers better what he writes or records in some way.
   (10) He can learn through vicarious experience as well as by firsthand experience.
   (11) He has some ability to discern time and space relationships but is basically oriented to the here and now.
   (12) He can work independently but often needs reminders to encourage him to complete individual assignments.
3. *Social*
   (1) He can accept simple rules, organization, responsibility, and leader/follower roles in group activities.
   (2) He is forming attitudes toward social groups, institutions, and authority.
   (3) He can recognize and appreciate individual differences among persons but sometimes does not include the "different" peer in his immediate circle of friends.
   (4) He gives evidence of changing attitudes toward the other sex and identifies more with his own sex.
   (5) He has a deep need for the companionship and approval

of his peers but continues to need adult approval and support.

(6) He is capable of recognizing and respecting the needs and rights of others but is motivated primarily by self-centered interests.

(7) He can operate with a degree of freedom and independence in a group.

(8) He is developing conscience, a value system, and characteristic behavior patterns.

4. *Emotional*

(1) He is learning to cope with success and failure.

(2) He is often a perfectionist about his work.

(3) He can enjoy trying to improve on his own achievements but often feels threatened by competition.

(4) He is ready for increasing responsibility and needs opportunities for self-direction and independent thinking.

(5) He is able to accept and work toward short-term goals.

(6) He achieves best in a climate of acceptance and encouragement and is easily discouraged.

(7) He feels deeply about his own experiences and can be sensitive to the feelings of others.

(8) He is easy to influence emotionally.

(9) His self-concept is developing, but usually he is unable to describe his feelings about himself.

(10) He is capable, with adult guidance, of experiences that involve imagination, deep feeling, and deep thought.

(11) He can identify and cope with some of his emotions.

(12) He has concepts of love and trust which strongly influence his feelings and actions.

5. *Spiritual*

(1) He can learn accepted limits for behavior in his world.

(2) He desires and intends to live up to his ethical standards.

(3) He is easily influenced as he develops values by which to live.

(4) He is developing a conscience and a value system.

(5) He finds it easy to love and trust God and Jesus un-

questioningly and to accept the Bible as a unique book.

(6) He is capable of experiences that involve deep thought and choice-making.

(7) He has a growing interest in spiritual matters that affect his life.

(8) He is developing a sense of right and wrong.

(9) He is forming concepts of his personal worth and can be helped by persons who love him.

(10) Many children this age do not realize that their sin and wrong doing is against God and that they should ask God for forgiveness.

(11) He can pray to God and can believe that his prayers are heard and answered.

(12) He is capable of putting into practice many Bible teachings.

(13) He asks many questions which have spiritual implications.

(14) He is capable of taking some responsibility for his behavior.

(15) His spiritual development is strongly influenced by his individual environment and experience and by other facets of his personal development.

(16) He begins to question the inconsistencies in people's lives who are Christians.

II. PURPOSEFUL OBJECTIVES IN TEACHING BIBLE DISCOVERERS

In our rapidly changing world, we need some constants. Our broad objectives in teaching children are such constants. Methodologists may come and go, but these objectives remain. They represent our long-range targets, the outcomes we hope to accomplish as the child grows, develops, and assimilates Bible truths.

The basic objectives may be grouped under seven major heads. Each heading indicates an area in which growth must come if a person is to achieve true spiritual maturity.

Because of individual differences among children, not all of the goals will be reached during the eighth and ninth years of every child's life. This is why "foundational teaching" becomes so important. Teachers of Bible Discoverers can lay foundations upon which other teachers may build, thus making possible the fulfillment of some of these objectives later in life.

Because of more rapid development or a greater number and variety of learning experiences, some children may proceed much further than others. We must remember that learning is an individual matter. We do not teach groups of children—we teach individuals. Some children are slower in development than others. They may be known as "late-bloomers." If we try to hurry the developing process, we usually hurt or bruise the one we are trying to help. Therefore, care should be taken to aid each child, realizing his growth rate is all his own and cannot be hurried.

Let us now examine each of seven major objectives with regard to the third and fourth graders.[4]

1. *Christian Conversion*

The teaching objective is to prepare each child for a genuine conversion experience when the Holy Spirit convicts him of his need to be saved from sin. Ways a Bible Discoverer can move toward the fulfillment of this objective are to:

- Feel love and reverence for God.
- Know that God loves him.
- Have a growing understanding of what the Bible says about right and wrong ways to think, feel, and act.
- Recognize that he needs God's help to do that which is right and good.
- Begin to realize the fact that the wrong things he does are sins against God.
- Grow in his understanding of what it means to forgive and that God wants to forgive him when he does wrong.
- Know that Jesus came to earth and died so that any person

---

[4] This presentation of objectives is based on information in *The Curriculum Base Design of The Sunday School Board of the Southern Baptist Convention*, Nashville. Tennessee. © Copyright 1974, The Sunday School Board of the Southern Baptist Convention. All rights reserved. Used by permission.

might receive God's forgiveness and salvation from sin.

- Understand that he receives God's forgiveness by turning from his sin and praying for forgiveness.
- Realize that becoming a Christian means that one turns from sin and asks God to forgive all his sin and to become the Lord of his life.
- Understand that a person becomes a Christian by trusting Jesus—not by being baptized and joining the church or simply by trying to be good.

2. *Church Membership*

The teaching objective is to help each child understand what is involved in being a church member.

3. *Christian Worship*

The teaching objective is to help each child develop the ability to participate actively and intelligently in worship and to find satisfaction in worship experiences.

4. *Christian Knowledge and Understanding*

The teaching objective is to help each child continually grow in knowledge and understanding of biblical truths which have meaning for his life. The objective is sought with respect to the Bible, the great realities of the Christian faith, the Christian movement, the local church, and the denomination.

5. *Christian Attitudes and Convictions*

The teaching objective is to help each child in the continuing development of attitudes and convictions that will encourage personal growth. We seek to help each child develop sound attitudes and appreciation regarding God, the meaning of existence, self, others, the Bible, divine institutions, and the present world.

6. *Christian Living*

The teaching objective is to guide each child to develop and use in everyday life habits and skills which will help him grow spiritually and will lay good foundations for Christian living after he has made Christ his Savior and Lord.

7. *Christian Service*

The teaching objective is to help each child use his talents and skills to serve God and help other people.

III. TOOLS FOR WORK WITH BIBLE DISCOVERERS

Third and fourth graders have special needs; and to meet these needs, materials are provided exclusively for this group. In this section we will look at the curriculum materials (lesson-course materials), provided by The Sunday School Board of the Southern Baptist Convention, at additional resource materials for workers, and at curriculum related filmstrips based on Bible stories and truths suitable for use with third and fourth graders.

1. *Curriculum Materials*

The lesson course materials cover various parts of the Bible which speak to the experiences of third and fourth grade children. Children of this age have experienced a limited range of emotions and problems. The development of the Bible material is influenced by the level at which children perceive their emotions and problems, by their school experiences, by their emerging concepts of time and space, and by their pattern of concrete thinking. Yet these children can be introduced to events in Bible history, to most of the major Bible characters, and to most of the major teachings of the Christian faith on a rudimentary level.

The narrative type of biblical literature is understood best by children of this age. Their understanding of narrative is limited chiefly by their vocabulary, though their life experiences may limit their perception of a narrative's implication. They have very limited understanding of the main thrust of poetry and prophecy involving symbolism, and they take most passages literally.

Bible Discoverers are beginning to understand the human motives which caused Bible people to behave as they did. Bible Discoverers are beginning to understand the obvious consequences of their own actions.

Children of this age are just beginning to place Bible people and events in chronological order or relationship. Therefore, the teaching materials place some emphasis on chronology, or sequencing, while still approaching Bible content by themes.

The curriculum materials for Bible Discoverers are planned

new each year. Careful consideration is given to provide balance, comprehensiveness, and progression. The basic objectives discussed earlier are foremost in the development of the curriculum plan. Some important factors concerning the curriculum materials are:

- Curriculum materials are Bible based.
- Curriculum materials are oriented to the age of the learner.
- Curriculum materials reflect sound educational principles.
- Curriculum materials are doctrinally sound.
- Curriculum materials writers are carefully chosen, are Southern Baptists, and work with the age group for whom they are writing.

The following periodicals are included in the Bible Discoverers series:

(1) *Bible Discoverers*

This pupil quarterly is designed for use at home and at Sunday School. The teaching units are interpreted month by month.

The Bible story and memory verse for each Sunday are printed in *Bible Discoverers*. Many units also include a short memory passage. Since children in the middle group are continuing to learn to handle their Bibles and are beginning to take responsibility for weekday Bible reading, the pupil's quarterly suggests weekly Bible readings. This section often includes interesting learning devices. Other games, puzzles, riddles, and picture activities are included for home use.

Bible Discoverers is a necessary item for Sunday morning learning experiences. Its maps, songs, articles, picture dictionaries, charts and diagrams, pretests, and illustrations provide information for research and other learning experiences in small and large groups. The teacher's quarterly frequently refers workers to materials in the pupil's quarterly.

Departments should provide a copy of *Bible Discoverers* for each teacher and pupil. If possible, order enough to have a few copies for use in the department on Sunday mornings and to replace those lost by pupils.

(2) *Bible Discoverers: Teacher*

This quarterly contains: (1) the kind of help teachers need for personal Bible study related to the units of study, (2) detailed information about how to guide the Bible-learning projects and activities each unit, (3) session-by-session suggestions for large group learning experiences, (4) lists of teaching aids and resources for each unit, and (5) resources such as songs, maps, and information needed for planning and evaluation. If a teacher has both a teacher's quarterly and a pupil's quarterly, he has at hand the essential teaching suggestions, information for research activities, Bible stories, memory verses, and songs.

Writers of *Bible Discoverers: Teacher* include ideas to help workers in departments with special needs (such as too many pupils per worker, space limitations. or pupils with a limited background in Bible study). The suggestions in the periodical regularly encourage workers to emphasize giving and church attendance. The development of skill in handling the Bible and other learning tasks faced by the middle-age child are provided for in teaching suggestions each week.

Every worker in the department should have a copy of *Bible Discoverers: Teacher* because all teachers and the department director are involved each week in providing Bible-learning experiences for children.

(3) *Teaching Pictures for Bible Discoverers*

This item is a quarterly set of ten full-color pictures explaining and illustrating the Bible stories and concepts of the quarter. In addition, at least three one-color pictures are printed on the picture backs in order to provide one picture for each session.

Information and teaching resources are printed on the backs of the other pictures in the set. These helps include songs, maps, fill-in charts, and games. *Bible Discoverers: Teacher* tells how to use the pictures and aids on picture backs.

A filing subject is assigned to each full-color picture. After each quarter, pictures should be filed by subject in a permanent department file. The filing system is described in a Program Help entitled *How Do I File My Pictures?,* available from the Materials

Services Department of The Sunday School Board.

Every department should order at least one set of pictures each quarter. If two sets can be ordered, helps on picture backs may also be filed by subject.

(4) *Resource Kit for Bible Discoverers*

This item is a quarterly kit of teaching aids designed to help workers save preparation time for themselves and do a more effective job of carrying out the teaching ideas in each unit. All kits are based on suggestions in *Bible Discoverers: Teachers*— games, maps, unit title banners, copies of Bible verses for display, choral-reading charts, questions for games, posters, puzzles for small groups to work together, individual information sheets, booklets, rebus activities, helps for teaching pupils how to find Bible references, and so on.

Every department needs at least one Resource Kit per quarter.

(5) *Adventure*

This weekly paper is designed for the Bible Discoverers to use for leisure reading and to reinforce the Bible story used each Sunday in *Bible Discoverers*. It includes at least one learning game or puzzle each week related to the Sunday morning Bible story as well as wholesome entertainment and character-building emphases not directly related to the curriculum. Use of the paper helps a child develop a positive attitude toward reading church-related materials.

In addition to a Bible emphasis each week, *Adventure* contains stories about real and fictional people and things, a poem, and suggestions for creative activities. The paper is well illustrated and is in full color.

Each child and each worker present should receive a copy each week. Additional copies should be ordered to mail to each prospect.

(6) *Children's Leadership*

This periodical is designed to assist the department director in administering the work of the department, to guide him in developing workers, and to help him interpret the Sunday School program in terms of the department with which he works. It also provides outreach projects with suitable suggestions for the outreach leader to use in implementing these plans. In addition, *Children's Leadership* provides help for Children's Division directors and for church staff members with responsibility for Children in Sunday School.

An important part of *Children's Leadership* is the planning section for workers with Bible Discoverers. Detailed suggestions are given for planning each unit of study in the quarter.

The department director, division director, outreach leader, Children's Worship leader, any church staff member with responsibility for Children's Sunday School work, and the pastor should receive a copy of the magazine each quarter.

2. *Resource Materials*

The following materials are helpful for workers with Bible Discoverers. They are available at the Baptist Book Store.

Blackwell, Muriel, *Outreach for Children.* Nashville, Tennessee: Convention Press, 1971.

Chamberlain, Eugene, *When Can A Child Believe?* Nashville, Tennessee: Broadman Press, 1973.

Fulbright, Robert G., *New Dimensions in Teaching Children.* Nashville, Tennessee: Broadman Press, 1971.

Ingle, Clifford, editor, *Children and Conversion.* Nashville, Tennessee: Broadman Press, 1970.

Bobbit, Paul and Leach, Bill F., editors, *Junior Hymnal.* Nashville: Tennessee: Broadman Press, 1964.

McElrath, William N., *A Bible Dictionary for Young Readers.* Nashville, Tennessee: Broadman Press, 1965.

McElrath, William N,. *Bible Guidebook.* Nashville, Tennessee: Broadman Press, 1972.

Rives, Elsie and Sharp, Margaret, *Guiding Children.* Nashville, Tennessee: Convention Press, 1969.

Songs for Children, Nashville, Tennessee: Broadman Press, 1964.

Stith, Marjorie, *Understanding Children*. Nashville, Tennessee: Convention Press, 1969.

3. *Curriculum-related Filmstrips for Use With Children*

(1) "Children's Resource Filmstrips"
- *Making Choices*
- *Church*
  Frames 1–18: What Do Churches Do?
  Frames 19–28: Church Helpers
  Frames 29–40: Learning Church Manners
  Frames 41–50: Worship Service
- *Bible Background*
  Frames 1–20: The Land of the Bible
  Frames 21–50: What Is the Bible?
- *Making Friends*
  Frames 1–15: Bible Friends
  Frames 16–26: What Makes a Good Friend?
  Frames 27–50: Learning How to Be Friendly

(2) "Children's Resource Filmstrips II"
- *The Christian Way*
- *Who Am I?*
- *Helpers*
- *We Learn Together*

(3) "Getting to Know God Better"
- *Getting to Know God through Jesus*
- *Getting to Know God through the Bible*
- *Getting to Know God through Prayer and Worship*
- *Getting to Know God through the World*

(4) *Home and Family Relationships*

(5) *Learning to Be Yourself*

(6) *The Story in the Bible*

(7) *The Land Where Jesus Lived*

(8) "Bible Story Series"
- *Jesus and His Helpers:* "Supper on a Hillside," "Philip the Missionary"
- *When the People Listened:* "Rules for Happy Living,"

"Ezra Reads the Scroll"
- *Dependable Joseph:* "Joseph and His Family," "Faithful Joseph"
- *God's Plan for Me:* "God's Care for Moses," "How Daniel Grew"

(9) "Bible Story Series II"
- *Jesus and His Life:* "Jesus the Boy," "Jesus the Man"
- *Story the Bible Tells:* "Old Testament," "New Testament"
- *Life of Paul:* "Early Life," "Missionary Journeys"
- *Friends of Jesus:* "Peter," "John," "Mary and Martha," "Lazarus," "Zacchaeus"

4. *Filmstrips for Use in Leadership Training*
   (1) *Teaching Bible Discoverers*
   (2) *Outreach for Unenrolled Children*
   (3) *Teaching Children the Bible*
   (4) *Using Music with Children*
   (5) *A Learning Environment for Children*
   (6) *Using Creative Dramatics with Children*
   (7) *The Preadolescent*
   (8) "Teaching Improvement Series: Children"
   - *The Adventure of Unit Teaching*
   - *These Are Your Children*
   - *You—a Worker with Children*
   - *Ways to Help Children Learn*

(Note: All of the listed filmstrips are produced by Broadman Films and are available at Baptist Book Stores.)

5. *Program Helps*
   (1) *Guidelines for Bible Study for Workers with Preschoolers and Children*
   (2) *How Do I File My Pictures?*
   (3) *Preschool and Children's Workers Witnessing*
   (4) *Your Child in the Sunday School*

(Note: Program Helps are available from Materials Services Department, 127 Ninth Avenue, North, Nashville, Tennessee 37234.)

IV. GROUPING BIBLE DISCOVERERS WITHIN THE DEPARTMENT

There are two kinds of groupings for Bible Discoverers—one is for home ministry and visitation, and the second grouping is for teaching in the small group on Sunday morning.

The first grouping for home ministry and visitation should be done at the beginning of the year or just prior to promotion time. The director or outreach leader will divide the names of the children equally among the workers in the department. Usually the children will be grouped by geographical areas and given to a teacher who lives in the same vicinity. Each teacher then visits each child in his group on a regular basis.

The second grouping establishes the small groups that are formed for each unit for the purpose of developing Bible-learning projects. Because learner needs are based on interest and involvement, children are given an opportunity the first Sunday of each unit to choose Bible-learning projects on which to work during the entire unit. Thus small groups are formed, consisting of two to seven children. These groups remain together for the unit. When the unit is culminated, the small groups dissolve. Then another new unit is introduced, other Bible-learning projects are chosen, and new small groups are formed. Therefore, the grouping for teaching Bible Discoverers is referred to as a temporary grouping.

Detailed help for introducing the unit of study and forming the temporary groups are given in the curriculum materials on a regular basis.

V. A BIBLE DISCOVERER AND HIS BIBLE

Children soon sense the importance and value placed on different things by adults. Daily newspapers come into the home, are read, and immediately disposed of. Library books are checked out to a reader, remain in his possession for a short time, and then are returned to the library, perhaps never to be read again. Classics are purchased—sometimes read—and placed on a bookshelf.

What message about the Bible is conveyed to the child? Is the Bible read regularly in his home? Is it used often in the department on Sunday morning? Is great care taken to introduce its important teachings to the children? Is the Bible the focal point for teaching in both small and large group?

Several versions of the Bible should be available in the Bible Discoverers department. A department Bible with large print and pictures is good to use in the large group while telling the Bible story or referring to Bible material. Opening the Bible while telling the story says to the children that the story is from the Bible. Voice inflections, facial expressions, and mood can convey the importance of the story felt by the storyteller. Underlining verses in the department Bible alerts children to gems of truth.

VI. BIBLE DISCOVERERS AND MEMORY VERSES

Bible Discoverers are encouraged to memorize a Bible verse each Sunday. Bible verses for children this age are carefully selected and printed in both teacher and pupil materials. As children begin to learn these verses, they begin to sense the importance of God's Word.

Let us think for a few minutes about the importance of memory work. Our language is a fascinating thing. We use the expression "learn by heart" to mean "learn word for word." But think a minute about the implications of learning by heart.

If one learns a truth by heart, he takes it into his inner being. He not only learns the words in their correct sequence; he learns the meaning of those words for his own life. Such a learner becomes emotionally as well as intellectually involved with what he gets down "word for word."

When thoughtful workers seek to help Bible Discoverers learn Bible verses, their deep concern is that children learn the verses "by heart"—even if they do miss a word here and there. To achieve this quality of understanding and involvement, workers must do more than encourage children to repeat words. Children must be helped to understand what they commit to memory if the memorized verses are to have their fullest effect. Children need more than a one-time interpretation of a verse if it is to become meaningful to them at the level which changes their lives. They need to experiment with applying the verse, its teaching as well as its words, in a variety of situations.

None of what has been said means that quoting the Bible accurately is not important. The importance of accurate quotation goes a lot deeper than the ability to grandstand through lengthy displays of Bible memory accomplishment. A third grader amazed his teacher with his ability to memorize Bible verses. Wishing to encourage him, the teacher pumped verse after verse into him with astonishing results. But when after a time the pupil attempted to repeat the blocks of Scripture he had learned, he altered the twenty-third Psalm to read, "My head runneth over." It did. If he had truly learned the psalm by heart as well as word for word, he might have quoted more accurately. The misquote was worth a chuckle to the alert listener, but the experience had little learning value for the boy.

VII. SUMMARY AND REVIEW

In Section B you have looked at:

- physical, intellectual, social, emotional, and spiritual characteristics of Bible Discoverers
- objectives in teaching Bible Discoverers
- tools for working with Bible Discoverers
- how to group Bible Discoverers for teaching and reaching
- how to help Bible Discoverers use the Bible
- how to help Bible Discoverers with memory verses.

In light of your experiences in the department in which you teach, take a moment to reflect on what you have read. Try to spot at least three things you will do as a result of your study of Section B.

Now you are ready to move to Chapter 4. That is, you are ready to move to Chapter 4 unless you want to explore distinctives about teaching and reaching Bible Learners or Bible Searchers.

Searching

I am ten straining for eleven;
And then Youth! Restless I push toward upcoming years,
Anxious to put off binding things of childhood,
Yet . . . unsure of leaving my somewhat sheltered world;
A world that has nurtured me on my voyage of why's.

A vagueness stirs within.
I do not yet know it as regret,
For the kaleidoscope focuses on unanswered why's,
Why's which diminish not but ever increase,
Exploding, fragmenting, forming new why's on the horizon.
And I continue to reach for answers.

I go this way but once.
This selfsame way I will not walk again.
So, you who teach,
Make my journey worth the while.

—Muriel F. Blackwell

SECTION C
BIBLE SEARCHERS

Asserting more independence than younger children, fifth and sixth graders are sometimes referred to as preadolescents. They have an extraordinary desire to learn. Their basic learning skills are refined to the degree that formal learning generally comes easy for them. Their ability to think logically and to look for cause and effect increases rapidly.

Even though some may reach puberty during these years, there is still the need and security of the familiar both from the home and the church. Fifth and sixth graders are beginning to face adulthood, and yet they have not turned their backs on childhood.

One of the most significant characteristics of Bible Searchers is the wide range of individual differences found within any group of them. Look at the findings in a survey of an actual sixth-grade class in a well-run school system:

The twenty-nine pupils show a range of more than 3½ years in chronological age, 104 pounds in weight, 14 inches in height, 62 points in IQ, and 8 years 4 months in mental age. Their achievement, as measured by the Iowa Every-Pupil Tests of Basic Skills, ranges from 4.3 to 9.9 in grade average, from 4.4 to 9.5 in reading and from 3.5 to 11.4 in spelling. In general, the oldest children in this class are the lowest in IQ and have the poorest achievement records. The brightest are about average in age for the grade and have the best achievement records. But a study of the individuals shows the effects of other factors than intelligence. A girl whose parents are on a high socioeconomic level is seventh in intelligence (IQ 110) but the first in level of language usage (grade 9.9). A boy with the same IQ, whose family immigrated shortly before he was born, has a grade level of 5.7 in usage but 7.1 in reading and 6.7 in arithmetic problems. The pupil, a girl, who has next-to-highest IQ (124) now ranks sixth on the grade average. Last year she ranked third and the year before, second—not a bad record, but her teacher knows she is bothered by her father's financial difficulties and that she has taken on heavy household duties because her mother is working.[5]

Even though these boys and girls appear to be well on the road to maturity, they still have many nurturing needs. The mobile society has forced many of their parents to sever ties with grandparents, aunts, and uncles. When his father is transferred to another state, a child has to begin all over again making new friends at an age when peer acceptance is critical. The instability of homelife creates additional problems for many children. Tensions brought about by broken homes tend to leave scars on children. Divided loyalties create conflicts. All of these factors point to the necessity for mature leaders in Sunday School.

Many fifth and sixth graders are entering a time zone in their lives during which serious consideration can be given to becoming a Christian. Boys and girls reach the age of responsible decision-making (age of accountability) at different chronological ages. For the first time, many fifth and sixth graders begin seriously considering the biblical requirements for becoming a Christian. The curriculum materials directly speak to this need.

Let us take a closer look at the group we are referring to as Bible Searchers. In many churches this group will be made up of fifth and/or sixth graders (ten and eleven year olds). In churches where there are few children, the Bible Searchers group may be composed of fourth, fifth, and sixth graders (nine, ten, and eleven year olds).

Fifth-grade department	Sixth-grade department
Fifth-and sixth-grade department	
Fourth-, fifth-, and sixth-grade department	

See Chapter 2 for detailed suggestions on how to organize your Bible Searchers department.

---

[5] Cutts, Norma E. and Nicholas Moseley, editors, *Providing for Individual Differences in the Elementary School.* Englewood Cliff, New Jersey: Prentice-Hall, Inc., 1960, pp. 1–2. Used by permission.

A Bible Searchers department serves the oldest children in the Children's Division. Workers with Bible Searchers build upon the foundations laid in the Bible Learners and Bible Discoverers departments. Because of the advance learning skills of this older group, they can be guided to do more depth Bible study through the Bible-learning projects and large-group learning. In addition to taking an active role in unit planning, Bible Searchers are involved in the detailed planning of the Bible-learning projects. Research, map study, and time lines are examples of the many kinds of learning activities in which this group is involved. (These and other methods are given in *Guiding Children,* Rives and Sharp.)

With concepts of time and space more fully developed than in earlier years and with an emerging appreciation for history, Bible Searchers can begin to grasp the full meaning of the biblical revelation. They can see how God has dealt with man down through the ages as recorded in the Bible. And because of this, the Bible Searchers curriculum plan presents every other year a chronological study of the Bible which begins in the book of Genesis, continues chronologically through the Bible, and ends in Revelation. Thus by the time he leaves the Children's Division, every child has had this overview of the entire Bible.

I. A LOOK AT BIBLE SEARCHERS

Good Sunday School teaching must begin where the person is. Only when each boy or girl is taken where he is and challenged to progress as far as he can go, will his achievement and the total achievement of the department approach the maximum. The teaching must be challenging enough to capture the learner's interest. As the learner becomes more involved, he utilizes his skills and knowledge. Therefore, understanding the children we teach is extremely important.

Time has a way of erasing from the memory of adults the trials and perplexities of fifth and sixth graders. Have you observed a teacher who had forgotten that fifth and sixth graders are talkative? Have you noticed that they forget easily and need to be reminded often? Or have you observed a teacher who forgot that boys and girls of this age cannot sit still for long periods of time? Or have you observed a teacher who had forgotten that boys of this age do not like to sit by or even associate with girls of this age and vice versa. Teachers who overlook the characteristics of Bible Searchers—what is normal conduct for them at this period in their lives—will not likely meet children's needs. These teachers often expect boys and girls to act like miniature adults. Normal behavior patterns of boys and girls may be interpreted as "mean" or "bad."

These pupil characteristics and the resulting learning readinesses dictate to the conscientious teacher the kind of physical space needed, the length of time blocks to be used in the teaching-learning process, the size of groups, the degree of interpersonal relationships that can be achieved, and the methods appropriate for the learner.

Therefore, understanding the following characteristics is extremely important in good Sunday School work with Bible Searchers.[6]

1. *Physical*

    (1) He is very active and moves about with great agility.

    (2) He is increasingly able to use his small muscles.

    (3) He has attained a good level of coordination and use of his motor skills.

    (4) He is eager to make use of his abundant energy and rapidly developing physical skills.

    (5) He needs occasional periods of inactivity.

    (6) He is approaching puberty, with the girl maturing more rapidly than the boy.

    (7) He can make full use of his eyes since eye muscle development is complete.

    (8) He can care for his own bodily needs.

---

[6] This listing of characteristics is based on similar lists in *The Curriculum Base Design of the Sunday School Board of the Southern Baptist Convention*, Nashville, Tennessee. © Copyright 1974, The Sunday School Board of the Southern Baptist Convention. All rights reserved. Used by permission.

2. *Intellectual*

    (1) He can make many types of choices but may not follow through on those which require long-term action.

    (2) He is ready to think for himself about things within his own realm of experiences.

    (3) He has some ability to express ideas, understand cause and effect, solve problems, reason, and plan.

    (4) He is capable of great concentration when interested and challenged.

    (5) He tends to think literally but is also capable of doing some abstract thinking.

    (6) He has limited skills in understanding figurative and symbolic language.

    (7) He has learned to use the basic academic skills (reading, writing, and so forth).

    (8) He learns quickly and is able to memorize easily.

    (9) He can employ imagination and creativity.

    (10) He demonstrates great curiosity and a wide variety of interests.

    (11) He can learn through vicarious experiences as well as by first-hand ones.

    (12) He is generally able to distinguish between fact and fiction.

    (13) He has some ability to discern time and space relationships, but is basically oriented to the here and now.

3. *Social*

    (1) He can accept simple rules, organization, responsibility, and leader/follower roles in group activities.

    (2) His attitude toward social groups, institutions, and authority is still rudimentary.

    (3) He can recognize and appreciate individual differences among persons.

    (4) He shows an intensified perception of sex roles, identifies more with his own sex, shows divergent interests according to sex, and gives evidence of changing attitudes toward the opposite sex.

(5) He has a deep need for the companionship and approval of his peers but continues to need adult approval and support.

(6) He is capable of recognizing and respecting the needs and rights of others but is motivated primarily by self-centered interests.

(7) He can operate with a degree of freedom and independence in a group.

(8) He can think and behave contrary to family influences which thwart his desire for independence and peer approval.

(9) He is developing conscience, a value system, and characteristic behavior patterns.

4. *Emotional*

(1) He is learning to cope with success and failure.

(2) He can enjoy trying to improve on his own achievements but may feel threatened by competition.

(3) He is ready for increasing responsibility and opportunities for self-direction and independent thinking.

(4) He is able to accept and work toward short-term goals.

(5) He achieves best in a climate of acceptance and encouragement but is easily discouraged.

(6) He feels deeply about his own experiences and can be sensitive to the feelings of others.

(7) He is easy to influence emotionally.

(8) His self-concept is developing, but often he is unable to describe his feelings about himself.

(9) He is capable of experiences that involve feelings, imagination, and deep thought.

(10) He can identify and cope with some of his emotions.

(11) He has concepts of love and trust which strongly influence his feelings and actions.

5. *Spiritual*

(1) He can learn accepted limits for behavior in his world.

(2) He desires to and intends to live up to his ethical standards.

(3) He is easily influenced as he develops values by which to live.

(4) He is developing a conscience and a value system.

(5) He finds it easy to love and trust God and Jesus unquestioningly and to accept the Bible as a unique book.

(6) He is capable of experiences that involve deep thought and choice-making.

(7) He has a growing interest in spiritual matters that affect his life.

(8) He is developing a sense of right and wrong.

(9) He is forming concepts of his personal worth and can be helped by persons who love him.

(10) He is beginning to realize that his sin and wrongdoing is against God and that he should ask God for forgiveness.

(11) He can pray to God and can believe that his prayers are heard and answered.

(12) He is capable of putting into practice many Bible teachings.

(13) He asks many questions which have spiritual implications.

(14) He is assuming more responsibility for his behavior.

(15) His spiritual development is strongly influenced by his individual environments and experiences and by other facets of his personal development.

(16) He is questioning the inconsistencies in people's lives who are Christians.

II. PURPOSEFUL OBJECTIVES IN TEACHING

In a rapidly changing world, we need some constants. Our broad objectives in teaching boys and girls are such constants. Methodologies may come and go, but these objectives remain. They represent our long-range targets, the outcomes we hope to accomplish as the individual grows, develops, and assimilates

Bible truths.

The basic objectives may be grouped under seven major heads. Each heading indicates an area in which growth must come if a person is to achieve true spiritual maturity.

Because of individual differences among children, not all of the goals will be reached during the tenth and eleventh years of every child's life. This is why "foundational teaching" becomes so important. Teachers of Bible Searchers will see some of these goals realized and can lay foundations upon which other teachers may build for the attainment of other goals in later years.

Because of more rapid development or a greater number and variety of learning experiences, some boys and girls may proceed much further than others. We do not teach groups of children—we teach individuals. Some individuals are slower in development than others. They may be known as "late-bloomers." If we try to hurry the developing process, we usually hurt or bruise the one we are trying to help. Therefore, care should be taken to aid each child, realizing his growth rate is all his own and cannot be hurried.

Now let us examine each of the seven major objectives with regard to fifth and sixth graders.[7]

1. *Christian Conversion*

The teaching objective is to prepare each boy and girl for a genuine conversion experience when he or she is competent to receive Christ as Lord and Savior and to lead to conversion each one who is ready. Ways Bible Searchers can move toward the fulfillment of this objective are to:

- Understand that all people do wrong and that all wrong-doing is displeasing to God.
- Face the fact that the wrong things which he does are sins against God.

---

[7] This presentation of objectives is based on information in *The Curriculum Base Design of The Sunday School Board of the Southern Baptist Convention,* Nashville Tennessee. © Copyright 1974, The Sunday School Board of the Southern Baptist Convention. All rights reserved. Used by permission.

- Realize that Christ's death for our sins makes possible forgiveness and new life for every person who repents of sin and trusts Jesus Christ.
- Understand that a person becomes a Christian by trusting Jesus—not by being baptized and joining the church or simply by trying to be good.
- Realize that he needs God's forgiveness for his own sins.
- Trust in Christ as his personal Savior and Lord when the Holy Spirit has made him ready for such response and commitment.

2. *Church Membership*

The teaching objective is to help boys and girls understand what it means to be a church member and to lead each Christian boy and girl into intelligent, active, and devoted membership in a New Testament church.

3. *Christian Worship*

The teaching objective is to help each boy and girl participate actively and intelligently in worship and find increasing satisfaction in worship experiences.

4. *Christian Knowledge and Understanding*

The teaching objective is to help boys and girls grow in Christian knowledge and conviction. The objective is sought with respect to the Bible, the great realities of the Christian faith, the Christian movement, the local church, and the denomination.

5. *Christian Attitudes and Convictions*

The teaching objective is to help each boy and girl develop Christian attitudes and convictions in every area of his experience. We seek to help each child develop sound attitudes and appreciations regarding God, the meaning of existence, self, others, the Bible, divine institutions, and the present world.

6. *Christian Living*

The teaching objective is to guide each boy and girl in learning skills and in developing habits which promote spiritual growth and Christlike conduct.

7. *Christian Service*

The teaching objective is to lead each boy and girl to develop and use his or her ability in worthy ways that will help others.

III. TOOLS FOR WORKING WITH BIBLE SEARCHERS

Fifth and sixth graders have special needs; and to meet these needs, materials are provided exclusively for this group. In this section we will look at the curriculum materials (lesson course materials) provided by The Sunday School Board of the Southern Baptist Convention, additional resource materials for workers, and curriculum-related filmstrips based on Bible stories and truths suitable for use with fifth and sixth graders.

1. *Curriculum materials*

The lesson course materials cover various parts of the Bible which speak to the experiences of fifth- and sixth-grade boys and girls. The development of the Bible material is influenced by the level at which children perceive their emotions and problems, by their school experiences, by their emerging concepts of time and space, and by their pattern of concrete thinking and limited ability to deal in abstracts. The boys and girls are introduced to major events of Bible history, to most of the major Bible characters, and to most of the major teachings of the Christian faith on a rudimentary level. Every other year, Bible Searchers make a survey of the Bible, beginning in the Old Testament and continuing through the New Testament.

The narrative type of biblical literature is understood best by children of this age. Their understanding of narrative is limited chiefly by their vocabulary, though their life experiences may limit their perception of a narrative's implication. They have a very limited understanding of the main thrust of poetry and prophecy involving symbolism, and they take most passages literally.

Bible Searchers are beginning to understand the human emotions which caused Bible people to behave as they did, and pupils are beginning to understand the obvious consequences of their own actions.

Bible Searchers have the ability to place Bible people and events in chronological order or in relationship. Therefore the materials involve chronology and sequencing.

The curriculum materials for Bible Searchers are planned new each year. Careful consideration is given to providing balance, comprehensiveness, and progression. The basic objectives discussed earlier are foremost in the devolpment of the curriculum plan. Some important factors concerning the curriculum materials are:

● Curriculum materials are Bible based.
● Curriculum materials are oriented to the age of the learner.
● Curriculum materials reflect sound educational principles.
● Curriculum materials are doctrinally sound.
● Curriculum material writers are carefully chosen, are Southern Baptists, and work with the age group for whom they are writing.

The following periodicals are included in the Bible Searchers series:

(1) *Bible Searchers*

This periodical is intended for pupils to use at the church and at home. Boys and girls are encouraged to read and reread the Bible stories and other features as often as they like. Using *Bible Searchers* helps boys and girls build an appreciation for the Bible.

The quarterly contains a Bible story for each Sunday. In addition, there are daily Bible reading suggestions taken from the Scripture passage for the coming Sunday. It also includes a memory verse or passage for each week. It suggests things to do at home related to the unit purpose. Other features are songs, short stories, and additional resource materials related to the unit purpose.

Every pupil and every worker in the department needs a copy of *Bible Searchers*. Enough additional copies should be ordered each quarter for new members, for prospects, and for replacement of lost quarterlies.

(2) *Bible Searchers: Teacher*

This periodical provides workers with the basic information they need in order to perform the task of teaching the Bible to boys and girls in their department.

Contents include session-by-session Bible study for the worker with suggested teaching procedures, as well as suggestions specifically related to each unit. Bible-learning projects for the small groups as well as large group procedures are included for each unit along with memory verses for each session. There are also articles of a general nature which the worker may wish to clip and save. Resources such as songs are a part of the periodical.

Each worker in the department needs to receive a copy of *Bible Searchers: Teacher* each quarter.

(3) *Teaching Pictures for Bible Searchers.*

This picture set provides enrichment for teaching-learning experiences in the department, both in the large group and in the small group. Each quarter the set contains ten pictures in full color. Some are photographs and some are paintings. Each picture is approximately twelve by seventeen inches in size and should be retained after the quarter and filed in a department picture file. Additional teaching suggestions are also included on the back of each picture.

A filing subject is assigned to each full-color picture. After each quarter, pictures should be filed by subject in a permanent department file. A good filing system is described in the Program Help entitled *How Do I File My Pictures?*, available from the Materials Services Department of The Sunday School Board.

Each department needs at least one set of teaching pictures each quarter.

(4) *Resource Kit for Bible Searchers*

This package of planned enrichment materials may be used in both large-group and small-group teaching. Such items as Bible-learning games, Bible-related puzzles, illustrated verses, recordings, and filmstrips may be included. Items are included that relate to each unit in the quarter.

Each department needs at least one Resource Kit each quarter.

(5) *Adventure*

This weekly paper is designed for the Bible Searcher to use for leisure reading and to reinforce the Bible story used each Sunday in *Bible Searchers*. It includes at least one learning game or puzzle each week related to the Sunday morning Bible story as well as wholesome entertainment and character-building emphases not directly related to the curriculum. Use of the paper helps a child to develop a positive attitude toward reading church-related materials.

In addition to a Bible emphasis each week, *Adventure* contains stories about real and fictional people and things, a poem, and suggestions for creative activities. The paper is well illustrated and is in full color.

Each child and each worker present should receive a copy each week. Additional copies should be ordered to mail to prospects.

(6) *Children's Leadership*

This periodical is designed to assist the department director in administering the work of the department, to guide him in developng workers, and to help him interpret the Sunday School program in terms of the department with which he works. It also provides outreach projects with suitable suggestions for the outreach leader to use in implementing these plans. In addition, *Children's Leadership* provides help for Children's Division directors and for church staff members with responsibility for Children in Sunday School.

An important part of *Children's Leadership* is the planning section for workers with Bible Searchers. Detailed suggestions are given for each unit of study in the quarter.

The department director, division director, outreach leader, Children's Worship leader, and staff member with responsibility for Children's Sunday School work, and the pastor should receive a copy of the magazine each quarter.

2. *Resource Materials*

The following materials are helpful for workers with Bible Searchers. They are available at Baptist Book Stores.

Blackwell, Muriel, *Outreach for Children*. Nashville, Tennessee: Convention Press, 1971.

Chamberlain, Eugene, *When Can A Child Believe?* Nashville, Tennessee: Broadman Press, 1973.

Fulbright, Robert G., *New Dimensions in Teaching Children*. Nashville, Tennessee: Broadman Press, 1971.

Ingle, Clifford, editor, *Children and Conversion*. Nashville, Tennessee, Broadman Press, 1970.

Bobbit, Paul and Leach, Bill F., editors, *Junior Hymnal*. Nashville, Tennessee: Broadman Press, 1964.

McElrath, William N., *A Bible Dictionary for Young Readers*. Nashville, Tennessee: Broadman Press, 1965.

McElrath, William N., *Bible Guidebook*. Nashville, Tennessee: Broadman Press, 1972.

Rives, Elsie and Sharp, Margaret, *Guiding Children*. Nashville, Tennessee: Convention Press, 1969

Songs for Children, Nashville, Tennessee: Broadman Press 1964.

Stith, Marjorie, *Understanding Children*. Nashville, Tennessee: Convention Press, 1969.

3. *Curriculum-related Filmstrips for Use with Children*

   (1) "Children's Resource Filmstrips"

- *Making Choices*
- *Church*
  Frames 1–18: What Do Churches Do?
  Frames 19–28: Church Helpers
  Frames 29–40: Learning Church Manners
  Frames 41–50: Worship Service
- *Bible Background*
  Frames 1–20: The Land of the Bible
  Frames 21–50: What Is the Bible?

- *Making Friends*
  Frames 1–15: Bible Friends
  Frames 16–26: What Makes a Good Friend?
  Frames 27–50: Learning How to Be Friendly
(2) "Children's Resource Filmstrips II"
  - *The Christian Way*
  - *Who Am I?*
  - *Helpers*
  - *We Learn Together*
(3) "Getting to Know God Better"
  - *Getting to Know God Through Jesus*
  - *Getting to Know God Through the Bible*
  - *Getting to Know God Through Prayer and Worship*
  - *Getting to Know God Through the World*
(4) *Home and Family Relationships*
(5) *Learning to Be Yourself*
(6) *The Story in the Bible*
(7) *The Land Where Jesus Lived*
(8) "Bible Story Series"
  - *Jesus and His Helpers:* "Supper on a Hillside," "Philip the Missionary"
  - *When the People Listened:* "Rules for Happy Living," Ezra Reads the Scroll"
  - *Dependable Joseph:* "Joseph and His Family," "Faithful Joseph"
  - *God's Plan for Me:* "God's Care for Moses," "How Daniel Grew"
(9) "Bible Stories Series II"
  - *Jesus and His Life:* "Jesus the Boy," "Jesus the Man"
  - *Story the Bible Tells:* "Old Testament," "New Testament"
  - *Life of Paul:* "Early Life," "Missionary Journeys"
  - *Friends of Jesus:* "Peter," "John," "Mary and Martha," "Lazarus," "Zacchaeus"
4. *Filmstrips for Use in Leadership Training*
  (1) *Teaching Bible Searchers*

(2) *Outreach for Unenrolled Children*
(3) *Teaching Children the Bible*
(4) *Using Music with Children*
(5) *A Learning Environment for Children*
(6) *Using Creative Dramatics with Children*
(7) *The Preadolescent*
(8) "Teaching Improvement Series: Children"
  ● *The Adventure of Unit Teaching*
  ● *These Are Your Children*
  ● *You—a Worker with Children*
  ● *Ways to Help Children Learn*

(Note: All of the listed filmstrips are produced by Broadman Films and are available at Baptist Book Stores.)

5. *Program Helps*
  (1) *Guidelines for Bible Study for Workers with Preschoolers and Children*
  (2) *How Do I File My Pictures?*
  (3) *Preschool and Children's Workers Witnessing*
  (4) *Your Child in the Sunday School*

(Note: Program Helps are available from Materials Services Department, 127 Ninth Avenue, North, Nashville, Tennessee 37234.)

IV. GROUPING BIBLE SEARCHERS WITHIN THE DEPARTMENT

An essential step toward effective Bible teaching with children is the grouping within each department. In Bible Searchers departments children are grouped differently from the way they are grouped in Bible Learners and Bible Discoverers departments. These differences are based on the boys' and girls' readinesses, their age-group characteristics, and their peer relationships.

Permanent groupings are suggested in Bible Searchers departments. Each small group should not exceed seven, with boys and girls grouped separately. Boys are grouped with a man teacher and girls are grouped with a woman teacher. These groups are for the purpose of Sunday teaching and also home ministry and visitation.

Why is the grouping with Bible Searchers different from the grouping in the younger departments within the Children's Division? Bible Searchers are separated by sex and permanently grouped because:

(1) During these later preadolescent years, boys and girls naturally group themselves by sex when given the opportunity. More effective group dynamics can be achieved when the group is made up of only one sex.

(2) Boys and girls of preadolescent years are assigned a teacher of the same sex because of the need for a good Christian model as sexual roles are being established and clarified. The physical changes occurring in the child's life prompt questions. These questions are usually asked more freely by a child when they are directed toward one of the same sex.

(3) Boys and girls of this age are seriously considering becoming Christians. Good rapport can be maintained better through a sustained relationship with one teacher over a period of months. If a boy or girl becomes convicted of sin or needs counseling, he more likely will feel free to seek help from a teacher with whom he has been closely associated during the year. In permanent groupings teachers will come to know the pupils better and will be able to detect those times when spiritual needs surface. Therefore, permanent groups pave the way for more effective evangelistic work with Bible Searchers.

V. A BIBLE SEARCHER AND HIS BIBLE

Boys and girls soon sense the importance and value placed on different things by adults. Daily newspapers come into the home, are read, and immediately disposed of. Library books are checked out to a reader, remain in his possession for a short time, and then are returned to the library, never to be read again. Classics are purchased—sometimes read—and placed on a bookshelf.

What message about the Bible is conveyed to the child? Is it read regularly? Is it used often on Sunday morning in the department? Is great care taken to introduce its important teachings to children? Is it the focal point for teaching in both the large and small group?

Several versions of the Bible should be available in the Bible Searchers department. Constant use of the Bible by workers in both the large and small groups signifies its importance. Voice inflections, facial expressions, and mood can convey the importance of biblical content being studied by the worker. Underlining verses in the Bible alerts boys and girls to gems of truth.

VI. BIBLE SEARCHERS AND MEMORY VERSES

Bible Searchers are encouraged to memorize a Bible verse each Sunday. In addition to Bible verses, blocks of Bible material should also be learned by fifth and sixth graders. The Bible verses for boys and girls of this age are carefully selected and printed in both teacher and pupil materials. As children begin to learn these verses, they can sense the importance of God's Word.

Let's think about the importance of memory work. Our language is a fascinating thing. We use the expression "learn by heart" to mean "learn word for word." But think a minute about the implications of learning by heart.

If one learns a truth by heart, he takes it into his inner being. He not only learns the words in their correct sequence; he learns the meaning of those words for his own life. Such a learner becomes emotionally as well as intellectually involved with what he gets down "word for word."

When thoughtful workers seek to help Bible Searchers learn Bible verses, their deep concern is that the boys and girls learn the verses "by heart"—even if they do miss a word here and there. To achieve this quality of understanding and involvement, workers must do more than encourage children to repeat words. Boys and girls must be helped to understand what they commit to memory if the memorized verses are to have their fullest effect. Bible Searchers need more than a one-time interpretation of a verse if it is to become meaningful to them at the level which changes their lives. They need to experiment at applying the verse, its teaching as well as its words, in a variety of situations.

None of what has been said means that quoting the Bible accurately is not important. The importance of accurate quotation goes a lot deeper than the ability to grandstand through lengthy displays of Bible memory accomplishment.

VII. SUMMARY AND REVIEW

In Section C you have looked at:
- physical, intellectual, social, emotional, and spiritual characteristics of Bible Searchers
- the objectives in teaching Bible Searchers
- tools for working with Bible Searchers
- how to group Bible Searchers for teaching and reaching
- how to help Bible Searchers use the Bible
- how to help Bible Searchers with memory verses

Take a moment to reflect on what you have read in the light of your experiences in the department in which you teach. Try to spot at least three things you will do as a result of your study of Section C.

Now you are ready to move to Chapter 4. That is, you are ready to move to Chapter 4 unless you want to explore distinctives about teaching and reaching Bible Learners or Bible Discoverers.

Chapter 4
Planning for Effective Reaching and Teaching

Reaching children for Sunday School and involving them in purposeful, life-changing Bible study doesn't just happen. It requires careful and deliberate planning by all of the workers within a Children's department. Committed workers sharing a common concern for reaching and teaching boys and girls must pay the price of careful planning if the objective is reached.

In this chapter, we will deal with the overall planning done by all the departments within the Sunday School; the annual planning needed by a Children's department; and, perhaps most important of all, the planning done week by week at the weekly workers' meeting by workers in individual departments.

Closely linked to planning is the scheduling of time in the department. How much time shall be used for small-group work? How much for large-group experiences? How shall we handle time on the Sunday we plan a unit as compared with the Sundays which follow in that unit? These are questions which department workers must face in planning. So this chapter also deals with department schedules. You can expect to get suggestions for the best use of time in the Sunday sessions of your department.

I. PLANNING WITH THE TOTAL SUNDAY SCHOOL

No Children's department can operate effectively in isolation from the other departments in the Sunday School. Each Children's department should be involved in planning the overall Sunday School program for the year. This planning is usually done in the Sunday School council. Each Children's department is represented on the council by its department director or, in larger Sunday Schools, by the Children's Division director.

1. *Undergird Churchwide Goals and Programs*

Children's departments are directly involved in the planning of a church's annual program of Sunday School work. Approximately 20% of the Sunday School enrollment in Southern Baptist Sunday Schools falls within the Children's Division. For this reason, it is most desirable that each Children's department undergird and support the plans projected by the entire Sunday School.

2. *Represent Children's Needs in Annual Planning*

Needs in the Children's Division should be identified and planned for at the Sunday School council level. At the annual planning stage (often when the church's calendar of activities is projected), the Children's Division director or department director(s) will present needs from the division. Some of these needs which should be planned for include:

- Presenting Bibles to first graders entering the Children's Division.
- Providing adequate literature for pupils, workers, and prospects.
- Furnishing the necessary supplies needed for Bible-learning projects.
- Budgeting funds to send workers to Glorieta and Ridgecrest for Sunday School leadership conferences and other

leadership training experiences.
- Determining the best use of available space and forecasting new departments that will be needed as enrollment goals are met.
- Projecting parent-worker meetings for the year.

II. DETERMINING WORTHY ANNUAL GOALS FOR THE DEPARTMENT

Setting department goals brings planning much closer home. At this point effective and realistic planning by workers can be done. This planning may be done during a workers' retreat, at an annual meeting at the church building, or in a worker's home. Even though all workers share and participate in the planning, the department director is responsible to see that planning is done. Annual planning is directly affected by the needs within the department, the leadership and resources available, and the commitment of the workers to quality Bible teaching for children. Following are some specific actions a department may consider in projecting annual plans.

1. *Adopt the "Children's Department Sunday School Achievement Guide" as a Planning Tool*

The Achievement Guide includes the basic elements of good Sunday School work with children. It becomes a checklist by which workers doing annual planning can identify strong and weak points in the department. There are three levels of recognition to be attained on the Achievement Guide: Merit Recognition, Advanced Recognition, and Distinguished Recognition. Free copies of the Achievement Guide may be ordered from your state Sunday School office or from The Baptist Sunday School Board.

2. *Set Enrollment and Attendance Goals for the Year*

Often in Sunday School work, we think only of our teaching responsibility. Yet a big area of Children's Sunday School work is outreach. What kind of strides will your department make this year in reaching new children and maintaining good attendance by those already enrolled? Set a challenging but realistic goal. Post the goal in your department room as a constant reminder. Set your goal in terms of net growth for the year.

	Now	Goal for one year later
Enrollment	21	28
Average Attendance	16	23

3. *Schedule In-service Training for the Department Workers.*

Improved teaching is dependent upon improved teachers. What can be done by the department to train its workers during the year? Project plans for the department workers to grow through such in-service training as:

- Regular Bible study (See the Program Help *Guidelines for Bible Study for workers with Preschoolers and Children.*)
- Book reviews, beginning with the basic study course books on Children's work
- Visiting an innovative public school classroom of the same grade you teach in Sunday School

4. *Plan for Children During the Week*

Annual department planning should provide for some contact with children during the week. Often Sunday teaching can be extended into homes if appropriate contacts are made. Sunday School workers should encourage children to participate in Training Union and in the music and missions organizations of the church which usually meet during the weektime. Children's Sunday School workers need to alert church leaders to other weektime opportunities for Bible teaching such as Vacation Bible School, Backyard Bible Club, and Weekday Bible Study.

5. *Plan for Parent Involvement*

One hour per week in Sunday School is not enough time to give a child the basic Christian education he needs. Therefore, teachers and parents are important partners in the teaching task. Plan to involve parents during the year. Of the many ways this can be done, a few are:

- Visit with a listening ear. A much clearer understanding of the child may be achieved through such visiting.
- In visiting share with parents ways they can use the Sunday School curriculum materials in the home. Encourage the reading of the Bible stories at home; suggest that memory verses be said at meal time; mention the possibility of working Bible games and puzzles as a family.
- Invite parents to visit the department one Sunday morning and experience the kind of Bible-learning the child is exposed to.
- Plan a parent-worker meeting at least one time during the year.

6. *Coordinate Work, Space, and Materials with Leaders of Children's Worship*

Plan ways to cooperate with the Children's Worship leaders if your church has a regular Children's Worship Service separate from the Adult worship service. Coordination of space, supplies, and equipment is especially needed. Plan for a smooth transition from the Sunday School hour to the Children's Worship Service.

III. MAINTAINING THE WEEKLY WORKERS' MEETING

1. *Project the Importance of Planning Weekly*

The weekly workers' meeting is a must if quality Bible teaching with children is to be sustained. The fact that teachers in a Children's department form a team and do cooperative teaching makes weekly planning mandatory.

2. *Schedule the Meeting in Harmony with the Total Sunday School*

The department planning is best done in conjunction with the weekly workers' meeting for the entire Sunday School. This meeting is usually held on Wednesday evenings; however, the day that the meeting is held is unimportant. The fact that it is held is critical.

Children's workers usually attend the general session to learn of promotional plans for the entire Sunday School and then go to their respective departments for planning. Three fourths (or the majority) of the time should be spent in the departments planning for Sunday. Even if there are only two workers in a Children's department, they need to meet each week and plan for the boys and girls whom they are to teach the following Sunday.

3. *Prepare Adequately for the Weekly Workers' Meeting*

As indicated earlier, the most important phase of the weekly workers' meeting is the time spent in planning in the department. The department director is responsible for this period. Good weekly workers' meetings must be carefully planned. With the many demands on people's time today, we cannot expect workers to attend a weekly workers' meeting unless they get specific help for teaching on Sunday morning.

The department director should use *Children's Leadership* as one of the basic sources for help in planning this meeting. Specific suggestions for each week are given in the magazine. A variety of planning actions will strengthen the meetings. There are so many good and helpful things that can be done at the weekly workers' meeting, the director will have no difficulty in offering variety.

In addition to the suggestions in *Children's Leadership* magazine, check the following listings of ideas for planning your weekly workers' meeting.

(1) *Activities to Be Done at the Weekly Workers' Meeting as a New Unit Is Being Introduced:*

_____ Evaluate the previous unit; discuss ways for possible improvement.

_____ Briefly survey the Bible material in the unit.

_____ Review and determine desirable outcomes for this unit.

_____ Select introductory activities for Sunday. Each teacher selects one for his group.

_____ Share large-group plans for Sunday.

_____ Identify possible Bible-learning projects for the unit.

_____ Consider ways to involve the children in planning the unit and selecting the Bible-learning projects.

_____ Learn the unit song and memory verses.

_____ Survey the Resource Kit items related to the unit and discuss ways to best utilize each.

(2) *Activities for the Weekly Workers' Meeting Related to Teaching*

_____ Evaluate the previous session.

_____ Discuss the why's of successes and failures.

_____ Review the desirable outcomes for the unit. What progress is being made toward achieving them?

_____ Study the Bible content for the unit.

_____ Identify the biblical truths that can be appropriated by the children through Bible-learning projects and large group activities.

_____ Determine materials and resources needed for Sunday.

_____ Assign responsibility for securing these materials and resources.

_____ Review books, articles, and leaflets pertinent to teaching children the Bible.

_____ View films, filmstrips, and other visuals on Children's work.

(3) *Activities to Be Done at the Weekly Workers' Meeting Related to Outreach.* (The outreach leader assumes responsibility for seeing that these actions are taken.)

_____ Assign each prospect to a worker in the department to be visited.

_____ Ask for reports on recent contacts with prospects and absentees.

_____ Share with workers the needs of children and home problems discovered in recent visiting.

_____ Report on progress toward the department's attendance and enrollment goals.

4. *Involve All Workers in the Weekly Workers' Meeting*

The success of the weekly workers' meeting is heavily dependent upon the participation of all the workers in the department. When a worker misses, the children he teaches are penalized.

Establish a high priority for the weekly workers' meeting. A commitment to the weekly workers' meeting at the time of worker enlistment will help to guarantee the success of good weekly planning.

Department directors have an obligation to the workers who attend to assist them in the preparation for the coming Sunday. A worker who knows that the time will be spent wisely and that he will be equipped for his teaching responsibility for Sunday will agree more readily to participate on a weekly basis. Plan to start and close on time and keep the discussion focused on the subject.

5. *Evaluate the Weekly Workers' Meeting*

How do you measure the success of a weekly workers' meeting? An effective weekly workers' meeting will result in reaching and teaching more children the Bible. It will equip workers in the following ways:

(1) Each worker will receive guidance in understanding and studying the Bible material for Sunday.

(2) Each worker will be more skilled in helping the children experience and express Bible truths through the Bible-learning projects.

(3) Through fellowship with other workers in the department, each worker will be strengthened in the Christian pilgrimage.

(4) Each worker will identify and secure materials and re-

sources needed for Sunday.

(5) Each worker will be able to identify his role and responsibility in the overall teaching plan for Sunday.

6. *Use Plan Sheets at the Weekly Workers' Meeting*

Plans important enough to be made on a weekly basis should be written. Writing plans for reaching and teaching clarifies ideas and makes them more specific. The form on which these plans are written is unimportant, but plans definitely need to be written. Using a unit plan sheet helps worker to cover the key areas of planning. There is less chance of overlooking an important planning element.

Following the planning meeting, each worker should have a written account of his responsibility, how he will approach his task, and the materials or resources he will need.

Following are unit plans sheets for each worker to fill out, each sheet containing specific information.

Unit Plan Sheet

(to be filled out by each worker in the department)

Unit title _____

Desirable outcome(s) _____

_____

_____

First Sunday

Small Group 1 (teacher)   Introductory Activity

_____   _____

Small Group 2 (teacher)

_____   _____

Small Group 3 (teacher)

_____   _____

Small Group 4 (teacher)

_____   _____

Unit Bible-learning Projects to Fulfill
Desirable Outcomes

Teacher	Project	Materials Needed
1. _____	_____	_____
2. _____	_____	_____
3. _____	_____	_____
4. _____	_____	_____

Large Group Plans

_____ , director

(Large group plans should include the Bible material, memory verse, music, methods of pupil involvement and resource materials such as the teaching pictures and Resource Kit items).

Session 1

_____

_____

_____

Session 2

_____

_____

_____

Session 3

_____

_____

_____

Session 4

_____

_____

_____

Small Group Plan Sheet

(to be filled out by each teacher leading a small group)

Bible-learning Project ——————— Teacher ———————

What is my desirable outcome for this Bible-learning project?
_____

What information di I need to lead the children in planning the Bible-learning project? _____
_____
_____

(to be filled in by teacher after involving pupils in small-group planning).

What do we want to learn through this Bible-learning project?
_____

How are we going to develop (make) this Bible-learning project?
_____

What will each person do on the Bible-learning project?

Name	Responsibility
_____	_____
_____	_____

What materials do we need for the next session? _____
_____
_____

What assignments need to be done and by whom? _____
_____

IV. SUNDAY MORNING SCHEDULE FOR CHILDREN'S SUNDAY SCHOOL DEPARTMENT

This planning chapter has been written assuming the following basic schedules for a Children's Sunday School Department are used. Because of the need for children to be involved in the planning of a unit, the schedule for the first Sunday of a unit is slightly different from the schedule for the other Sundays of a unit. Generally the study units are a month in length. This fact means that on the first Sunday of the month you will follow the first schedule; the other Sundays of the month you will follow the second schedule.

A department must of course operate on the same overall schedule as does the rest of the Sunday School. Many churches allot only one hour to Sunday School. Others, realizing how important ten or fifteen minutes more may be in the teaching-learning process, allot more time. The schedules reflect these differences. Happy is the department which has the maximum time.

Schedule for the First Sunday of a Unit

15–20 minutes—*Small Groups* (Each small group participates in an introductory activity, usually in the form of a learning game, Bible puzzle, or a similar device related to the Bible content of the unit.)

30–35 minutes—*Large Group* (The Bible material for this session is presented, along with an overview of the unit. Desirable outcomes are shared with the group, and the Bible-learning projects to be done by each small group are identified and planned. Specific guidance for unit planning is given in the teacher periodicals.)

15–20 minutes—*Small Group Planning* (Each small group

makes detailed plans on how its Bible-learning project will be developed, how each member of the small group will be involved, and so forth. Specific guidance for small-group planning is given in the teacher periodicals).

Schedule for the Other Sundays of a Unit

35–45 minutes—*Small Groups* (As each small group meets with a teacher, work is done on the Bible-learning projects. Bible material for each Sunday is discussed and expressed through the Bible-learning project.)

25–30 minutes—*Large Group* (The small groups come together, forming a large group. The department director serves as teacher. Music, prayer, conversational teaching, Bible materials are all used. Involvement techniques are employed by the director. NOTE: On the last Sunday of the unit the large group time includes each small group's reporting its Bible-learning project and verbalizing Bible materials learned.)

V. SUMMARY AND REVIEW

To make your study of this chapter most meaningful, try to answer each of the following questions thoughtfully.

1. What is the one single greatest weakness in the planning done by the department in which you work?

2. What immediate step could be taken to offset this weakness?

3. What tools have you found in this chapter which may be of use in your department's planning?

4. In light of 'the information concerning schedules, how wisely has your department been using its time?

Chapter 5
Using Weekday Opportunities to Meet Needs

One young child thought that his Sunday School teacher lived in the church house. He saw her every time he went to the church. And as far as he knew, she had no existence apart from the hour and fifteen minutes he saw her on Sunday morning.

Too many Sunday School teachers seem to feel that Sunday morning is their only opportunity to meet the needs of boys and girls. This chapter will help you explore ways in which you and your fellow workers can use weekday opportunities to help boys and girls as well as their parents. Read it carefully and adapt its suggestions to improve the quality of your work.

A Children's Sunday School department is truly a place where the statement that everybody is somebody comes true. As you noticed in the chapter dealing with organizing to teach and reach children, every boy and girl, whether a member or a prospect, is the direct responsibility of some worker. Each teacher in the department has a small group of pupils with whom he seeks to build a special relationship through contacts outside the Sunday School hour as well as through the exciting things they do in the department on Sunday morning.

A department's prospects are also assigned to workers for cultivation. The assignment is made as soon as a prospect is discovered.

Between assigned pupils and assigned prospects each worker has a number of boys and girls and families with whom he should deal in one way or another each week. The ways in which he deals with these children and their families and the things which he seeks to achieve are what this chapter is all about. In the main, we can say that he will visit them in their homes from time to time for a variety of purposes and he will minister to them as persons and families. Let's take a closer look at the major phases of his work which go on all week long.

I. A SUNDAY SCHOOL WORKER IS A VISITOR

What is your attitude toward visitation? Do you sometimes wish that someone would come up with a new word for this— well, what do you want to call it? Are you tired of being told that you *ought* to visit in the homes of your pupils? Have you memorized all the reasons for making such visits?

If you answered yes to most of the questions in that paragraph, you just may be able to read this entire section without a single new thought. On the other hand, you may gain some fresh insights into this important all-week-long activity.

If you have no preconceived ideas about visitation, reading this section should be a pleasurable experience for you. Let it help you think through your own responsibility.

1. *Visit to Get Acquainted with Children*

Visitation is imperative in getting to know children well enough to guide their spiritual development. While get-acquainted visitation may be spread through the year and may be achieved in a variety of ways, let's take a closer look at two such visits.

One visit we will examine is a visit to an enrolled child. The other visit we will look at is a visit to a prospect.

Beginning a new Sunday School year with as much information as possible about each child is important. So a visit prior to Promotion Day is in order. As soon as department workers know the names of the children who will be assigned to their department for the new year, they should determine which children will be the responsibility of which teacher. (The chapter on organization deals more fully with this matter.)

As soon as assignments are made, a teacher is ready to visit the children assigned to him. If it is not possible to visit each child prior to Promotion Day, the teacher should set a definite date by which he will have visited with each pupil. The earlier in the year that this work is completed, the better.

Since it is quite likely that the teacher has never been in these particular homes before, he may wish to call ahead before making each visit. Many families appreciate some warning. Too a call saves the worker's time if families are not at home.

What can you as a teacher do on this first get-acquainted visit? Obviously, you will introduce yourself to the parents and to the child as his new teacher. Try to establish a link with the child, rather than with the whole family on this visit. One way to do so is to take the child his new pupil's quarterly. Since little things often count for a lot, be sure his name is on the quarterly and be ready to tell him how you expect him to use the quarterly. Avoid, however, making your expectations sound like school assignments. Try to help the child understand how his quarterly is arranged. Point out what you will be learning about during the first few weeks of the new year. Share your own excitement about what you will be studying together.

You may want to use an information sheet as a way to get better acquainted. In as far as possible, the pupil himself should complete the form. Of course, in the case of younger children, you will have to do most of the writing. However, don't overlook a child's ability to manuscript write at least his own name. And don't rush him. The questions on the form will hopefully

INFORMATION SHEET

Children's Sunday School Department

(To be filled out by pupil)

Name _____ Grade _____

Address _____ Phone _____

What school do you attend? _____

Age _____ Date of Birth: Mo. _____ Day _____ Year _____

Christian _____ Church member _____ Member of

what church? _____

Do you have brothers and sisters? _____ If yes, what

are their names and ages? _____

_____

What is your hobby? _____

Favorite TV show? _____

(To be filled out by pupil's parent/guardian)

Parent's (guardian) name _____

How long has your child been enrolled in Sunday School? _____

Does he attend Sunday School regularly? _____

Father a Christian? _____ Member of what church? _____

Mother a Christian? _____ Member of what church? _____

Enrolled in Sunday School: Father? _____ Mother? _____

Brothers? _____ Sisters? _____

Daily Bible reading and prayer in the home? _____

Father's occupation _____

Mother employed? _____ Where? _____

Will you encourage your child to be a regular attender of Sunday School?

_____ Do you need transportation to and from church? _____

Is your child a Christian? _____ If so, is he/she a

church member? _____ Where? _____

Additional information? _____

Dates of visits in home (by teacher) _____

_____

_____

stimulate conversation through which you will learn more about the child than his answers alone would reveal.

Now what about an initial visit to a prospect and his family? As in the initial visit to an enrolled child and his family, your primary purpose is to get acquainted. However, shoving some sort of form at prospects is not the better part of wisdom. Just how the child came to be a prospect plays an important part in what you should do in the initial visit. If the child has visited in your department, you may already have given him a quarterly. He has at least become aware of what your Sunday School time together is like. If his name, or his family' name, has been picked up from some source such as a community welcoming service, he probably knows almost nothing about you or your church.

Share with the child and his family what Sunday School is like and what it means to you. Try to help them feel that Sunday School has something to offer each of them, particularly the child you are visiting. Avoid leaving the impression that you just ran by to invite them to Sunday School. Show real interest in them as persons.

A good way to interpret the Sunday School setting is to take the child a current copy of the pupil's quarterly which the child will use if he comes to your department. If your department cannot afford quarterlies for prospects, then take along a copy of *More* or *Adventure*. Be sure the child and his parents understand that this piece is not a Bible study guide. For the sake of parents, take along a church bulletin or church paper. Or perhaps your church has a special brochure for sharing with newcomers.

On this initial visit, be tactful. The pastor of a large city church arrived at a home where the moving van was still being unloaded. He said to the woman who stood on the porch, "I am your new pastor."

"Not mine," was her quick reply. And surely enough he never was. One wonders what might have happened if he had offered to help or if he had waited a day or so until the woman was ready to receive visitors.

Do try to learn as much as you can about the family. This information will help you and others to build a good relationship with the family. As soon as you leave the home, record the information. Perhaps you can use a form such as the one included here.

PROSPECT INFORMATION

Child's name _____

Address _____ Phone _____

Age _____ Date of birth: Mo. _____ Date _____ Year _____

Grade _____ School _____

Parents' Name _____

Parents prospects for _____ Adult Sunday School Dept.

Information about parents _____

Additional Information _____

_____

Dates of visits in home:

A good way to conclude this initial visit is with an offer to take the family to Sunday School and to the worship service of your church. Many newcomers feel much more comfortable if they do not have to go into a strange church alone.

After the visit, follow through on the procedure your Sunday School uses to enlist new persons. If this procedure requires completing certain forms and sending them to certain persons, do this bit of record-keeping immediately.

2. *Visit to Develop Friendships with Children*

"Mother, it's my teacher." The six-year-old's reaction was somewhat like Rhoda's reaction when Peter appeared at the doorway of that home in Jerusalem. He was so excited that he wanted to share the news even before he invited his guest into the living room.

Continuing visits to the homes of the children one teaches help to build that bond which is so important in the teacher-pupil relationship. But this relationship is built best when a child feels his teacher is visiting him, not his parents.

3. *Visit to Encourage Children in Bible Study*

Each quarter provides a built-in opportunity to visit children to encourage them in Bible study. Every three months each child on your group should receive a new quarterly. Frequently workers simply hand out new quarterlies as children attend Sunday School. Sometimes quarterlies which are not picked up in this way are mailed to members and prospects. A better way to handle quarterly distribution is to deliver them to the homes of pupils.

Dashing by a home and sticking a quarterly hastily into a child's hand is of course little better than handing him the book when—and if—he shows up for Sunday School. Except of course it does make sure that the quarterly is in his possession at home.

Consider these ideas for use as you deliver a quarterly to a pupil:

- Talk with him about the first unit of study, letting him feel your own excitement.
- Review with him how to use his quarterly to best advantage. Show him how he can use it for home study. Review such features as guidance for daily Bible reading.
- Help him determine a plan for individual study. Maybe you can suggest that he keep his Bible and quarterly by his bed or on a desk in his room where they will be handy.
- Work one puzzle or play one game from the quarterly with him. Encourage him to share how he feels about what he is presently doing in Sunday School and to make sug-

gestions for improving what he is doing at home or at church.

- Share a simple testimony about the value of Bible study in your own life.
- Deal with questions he has about the things he has studied or about the Bible and the Christian life in general. You may not have all the answers, but you can let a child know that you are ready to try to help him. Remember that you have given a child a priceless gift if you have helped him to develop a love for Bible study and to build habits of regular Bible study.

4. *Visit to Help Children under Conviction*

When a worker realizes that a child he teaches is under conviction for his sins, the worker should make himself available for individual counseling. A visit to the child is indicated. Worker and child need a private time together during which the worker can help the child understand what his experience means. While the worker avoids pressuring a child to a premature decision, he can present the claims of the gospel clearly and simply. The child can respond with his own comments and questions, gaining the insight and understanding he so vitally needs at this point in his life. This visit should be made with the knowledge and consent of the child's parents, and they should be informed of the results of the visit.

5. *Visit to Get Acquainted with Parents*

If a person retreats into working with children because he doesn't like to deal with adults, he may be kidding himself about the real nature of Children's work. Whenever one becomes involved with children, he becomes involved with parents. You don't have to be an adult specialist, capable of teaching Bible at adult level or counseling parents at a professional level. You do need to be willing to become a friend to parents.

And friends are people who care enough about you to come to see you from time to time. As parents feel a bond growing with you, they become increasingly able to entrust their children to you. They become more and more eager for their children to be with you in Sunday School.

6. *Visit with Parents to Discover Children's Needs*

One of the best ways to discover the needs of children is to visit with their parents and discuss the children. There are few parents who do not want to talk about their children. While most parents are not objective about their children, they are still the best single source of information and insights into their children.

Challenging a parent with a problem which his child presents to you is seldom tactful. Who wants a visitor who says: "You've got to do something about the way Johnny behaves. He is tearing up my department."

On the other hand, a parent appreciates a visitor who says: "I'm interested in understanding Johnny better so I can do a better job of teaching him. What can you tell me about how he feels about what we are doing in our department?"

In the course of discussion, you may be able to share insights which will help the parent in his task of rearing the child. Remember, however, that few Sunday School workers are professional counselors or child psychologists. A parent has every right to reject advice you may freely hand out. Planting a seed of an idea is usually a better idea than giving blunt instruction about how to handle the child.

It is important not to let ideas from such discussions get away. As soon as possible after a visit, make some notes. If you are keeping information sheets such as the one in this chapter, your insights could be recorded on the back of the pupil's sheet.

7. *Visit to Win Lost and Unchurched Parents*

"A Christian home for every child." Can you think of a more significant slogan? The best thing you can ever do for a child is to help him have a Christian home. In this way the Christian teaching and training which the child receives on Sunday morning are reinforced and extended throughout the entire week. The first objective of a teacher in relation to non-Christian parents should be to win them to a saving belief in Jesus Christ.

An effective witness to lost parents requires more than one

pop-in visit. The parents' confidence and trust must be developed over a period of time. The parents must become aware of what your own faith means to you. From the very beginning of the relationship, plan ways to give your testimony.

Working under the guidance of the Holy Spirit when you feel the time is right, talk directly with the unsaved parent about his relationship to Christ. At this time you will likely want to show him marked passages in a Bible, passages which will help him realize his true spiritual condition and what he must do in order to be saved. A good modern translation of the New Testament will likely be helpful.

Parents who are Christians but not members of a local congregation need to become active participants in the Christian community. Your testimony about the significance of your church in your life is important in helping them realize their own need. Parents pick up subtle clues from chance remarks. For instance, if you refer to what "they" are doing at the church, parents are not likely to feel that you are deeply involved with the people in your church—even if you go regularly and even if you are a teacher in the Sunday School.

8. *Visit to Strengthen Family Worship*

If you use the suggested information sheet, you will know whether or not a family is engaging in daily family worship. Make either *Home Life* or *Open Windows* available to families which need resources for worship. Rather than simply handing either publication to a parent, take a moment to show him how to use it. Never forget that regular family worship strengthens parents for guiding children in their spiritual development.

II. A SUNDAY SCHOOL WORKER MINISTERS TO PARENTS AND CHILDREN

Someone has said that to minister to another is to do for that person what Christ would do if he were present in the flesh. We cannot do precisely what Christ might do were he present

with us in the flesh. We cannot raise a beloved son from the
dead as Jesus did for the widow at Nain (Luke 7:11–17). Nor
can we by our touch or words give power to impotent legs as
Jesus did (Luke 5:17–26). We cannot drive out evil spirits and
restore a tortured mind to sanity as Jesus did for the Gadarene
demoniac (Luke 8:26–39).

Perhaps it would be better to define ministry a bit differently.
Acting because of the great love and compassion which Jesus
revealed and has bestowed upon us, we become channels
through which his love and compassion flow into the lives of
persons around us.

1. *Minister in Times of Family Crisis*

What are the crises which families face in which they particularly need to be aware of God's love? You could easily list
at least some of these crises from your own personal experience.
Let's look at a few common crises. Then we can look at some
of the things which a worker can, often in cooperation with
other department workers, do for families in such times.

(1) *Illness.*—Illness, particularly illness involving hospitaliza-
tion of a family member, is always a crisis. Regardless of confidence in its doctor and regardless of its health insurance, a
family rarely faces serious illness calmly. Schedules are dis-
rupted. There may be some feeling of "why did this happen to
us." Children inevitably feel the tensions of their parents.

(2) *Death.*—Adults may accept with comparative calm the
loss of a family member such as a grandparent. But children
may be bewildered by normal grief, for death is a new experience for them. When death comes even closer as in the loss
of a husband or wife, the father or mother in the home, the
crisis becomes more acute. Even the death of a close family
friend may awaken strong feelings which give a child real
difficulty.

(3) *Divorce or separation.*—In recent years divorce and
separation have increasingly devastated even Christian families.
Regardless of what one may think about the rights and wrongs
of a given divorce or separation, such an experience always

disorients family members. All of them need the support of persons who sincerely care for them.

(4) *Loss of job.*—Losing a job, whether the loss results from impersonal economic trends, from personal misconduct, or from professional incompetence, is demoralizing. Persons caught in such experiences and these immediately around them need assurance of their personal worth—to God, to others, and to themselves.

(5) *Loss of home.*—Some psychologists tell us that every person needs a bit of space which is truly his. When fire, flood, or economic conditions force people from the space which they have regarded as their own, they suffer. They may even feel that they are being punished for sins, real or imagined.

(6) *Family triumphs.*—We are so accustomed to thinking of crises in a negative sense that we sometimes fail to realize that good fortune can be a crisis too. But we must not forget the scriptural admonition to rejoice with those who rejoice (Rom. 12:15).

Here are some of the more common instances of good fortune which may befall the families of children you teach. In each instance, you have the opportunity to provide Christian support.

- A new home may represent the culmination of many dreams and much planning.
- A new job may lead a family to develop a different life style.
- A new baby usually brings joy. But even a welcomed baby brings changes, changes which are sometimes painful to older brothers and sisters.
- Special recognitions often change the status of an individual or a family and can bring changes in the home. Recognitions may come to children for academic or athletic excellence. Recognition may come to a wife or husband for professional excellence.

2. *Minister in Many Ways*

To act in Christ's stead in response to human needs involves many different types of actions. We shall look together at only a few which seem most frequently to be the means by which Children's workers can convey the love of Christ and the support of the church.

(1) *Listening.*—It seems almost inane to emphasize the importance of being available as listeners to people in crisis. Yet listening is one of the most significant services Christians can perform for others. People in grief and people in triumph all need to express their feelings aloud to someone who has the patience to listen. Many times the listener can help such a person handle his strong feelings well even if the listener says not one word. Of course, the good listener does frequently have opportunity to offer tactful advice.

(2) *Providing services.*—When our friends face crises, we frequently ask, "Is there anything I can do for you?" And almost invariably the answer is, "No." For this reason, some say we should seldom ask the question at all, but should instead look about for something to do and do it. Consider these possibilities for helping families of members and prospects in times of crisis:

- Take meals to the home or provide for meals elsewhere.
- Supply needed clothing or handle necessary washing, ironing, and clothing repairs.
- Provide needed economic resources or help family members find work.
- Take family members into your home or arrange needed housing.
- Make telephone calls which upset family members would otherwise have to make.
- Offer to care for children of the family, in their home or in yours.
- Take over household routines, such as cleaning, which family members may not presently be able to perform.
- Run necessary errands such as grocery shopping, taking children to music lessons, and picking up medicines.

3. *Use Resources for Ministry*

Likely your department workers simply respond in a natural way to instances of family crisis among its members and prospects. There is, however, a subtle temptation to overlook quieter forms of crisis such as continuing illness. For this reason, *Children's Leadership* frequently carries plans for setting up a continuing ministry by department workers. Review this quarterly publication for suggestions.

Basically, each plan involves a few simple steps. Department workers survey their members and prospects to determine which persons or families need acts of ministry. Then workers select the most appropriate actions and assign responsibility for taking such actions. These actions are later reported to all workers, and needed next steps are determined.

III. A WORKER INVOLVES PARENTS AND PUPILS THROUGH THE WEEK

As natural outgrowths of the relationships established in Sunday School, workers involve pupils and their parents in many kinds of weekday activities. Each of these activities is purposeful, and each can be tailored to specific needs. As you examine the possibilities in this section, you may discover some ideas for use with your own group or department.

1. *Service Projects*

Many units of study lead naturally to doing something for someone else. How appropriate it is for a group of children to visit a shut-in or to prepare a book for a children's hospital as they study a unit which deals with ministry. As a rule, suggestions for appropriate service projects will be found in the teacher's curriculum materials.

When a crisis arises in the church family in which children can truly help, how appropriate that boys and girls should do what they can. For instance, children can help a friend who must be out of school over an extended period of time.

2. *Special Events*

Picnics, game parties, seasonal parties, and athletic events (church and school) give teachers and pupils chances to share another type of experience. Genuine fellowship builds as people engage together in such activities.

3. *Parent-worker Meetings*

From time to time most departments can help families by providing get-togethers focused on children, parents, and their needs. Such times enable workers to explain to parents what they are trying to do for the children and let both parents and workers explore how they may all more effectively work to help the children entrusted to them.

Parent-worker meetings take a variety of forms. They range from individual conferences, scarcely more formal than a drop-in visit, to joint meetings in which guest speakers with special qualifications deal with some aspect of parenting or Bible teaching. A popular type of meeting is an open house in the department room. The children and workers are hosts for the sharing of projects and Sunday procedures.

Curriculum materials provide many helps for workers interested in using parent-worker meetings to help parents. Some suggestions appear from time to time in teacher materials. Other suggestions appear frequently in *Children's Leadership*.

IV. A WORKER USES MANY METHODS TO KEEP IN TOUCH WITH FAMILIES

So far in this chapter we have talked about face-to-face times in which a worker is with either parents or children. There are other means by which a worker can keep in touch with and be of help to families.

One of these means is the telephone. Few children receive many personal telephone calls, particularly from adults. Children are more than pleased to hear, "This call is for you." Telephone calls can assure absentees of your interest in them. Telephone calls can let a worker remind pupils of assignments they have accepted in small-group work. Telephone calls can remind pupils of daily Bible reading.

Cards and letters provide another way to keep in touch. Only a lazy worker, however, uses cards and letters week after week as a substitute for visitation in homes. You may tell a person what you want him to know by means of a card. But you learn little about parents or children by means of cards you send them.

A card or a letter should be highly personal. A ready-made message may be better than none at all. But ready-made messages are rather impersonal. When writing a card or letter, make your message specific. Be sure, too, that your writing is legible enough for the child to read. Manuscript writing is a good idea even for older children since cursive writing is frequently extremely difficult for children to read.

A message by card or letter is more effective if it has a "hook." One teacher in a department for older children sent each of his boys a letter one week. The letter reminded them of assignments they had accepted. And each letter also contained a rubber band, but no comment about it. The very next Sunday the boys were in Sunday School, full of curiosity about the meaning of the rubber bands. Had the bands happened into the letters by accident or were they to serve a definite purpose, they wanted to know. Of course, the bands had already served their purpose.

Newsletters offer another means of communication. One department sends a newsletter to the home of every member and prospect once each quarter. The letter explains to parents the units to be studied during the next three months. It also describes interesting activities in which the pupils have engaged during the current quarter. Announcements about church activities of interest to parents are included. Other departments issue newsletters from time to time as workers feel special need for such communication.

V. A WORKER SUPPORTS OTHER BIBLE STUDY OPPORTUNITIES

What is the dream of every Sunday School teacher of boys and girls? Is it not something like this: to help each pupil become a true student of the Bible with a continuing interest in exploring its depth and in applying its truths to his life. With such a dream, each teacher becomes concerned with all the Bible study opportunities which his church offers to children. In this chapter we will look at some Bible study opportunities other than Sunday School which churches commonly offer to children.

1. *Church Vacation Bible School*

The Vacation Bible School which a church offers annually at its own building is perhaps the best established extension activity of the Sunday School. The first such school conducted by Southern Baptists was held more than half a century ago. Year after year the number of boys and girls, grades 1–6, involved in Vacation Bible School has continued to grow, until that number now exceeds the 920,000 mark.

Vacation Bible School is important because of its wide appeal. It is even more important because of the opportunities it provides for Bible study and related activities. Estimating the impact of ten consecutive three-hour sessions is difficult, but we know that the effects of Vacation Bible School are long lasting. Many an adult can tell you how meaningful these early experiences were in his life.

New curriculum materials are provided each year for all departments in Vacation Bible School. In the Church Series, new Children's materials are provided at the three levels for which materials are provided in Sunday School: younger, middle, and older children. These materials are correlated with other materials from Sunday School, Training Union, Church Music, and mission organizations. These materials are sold through Baptist Book Stores, and each year's materials are made available about January 1.

Each Sunday School worker must ask himself just what his own involvement in Vacation Bible School should be. If he does not serve on the Bible School faculty, he can still encourage boys and girls to participate. He can speak favorably of the school to parents and other adults. He can sometimes help the Bible School faculty as it prepares for its work. And he can most certainly participate in following through on children who are discovered as prospects for his department through the Vacation Bible School.

2. *Mission Vacation Bible School*

A mission Vacation Bible School does not usually offer a Bible study opportunity to the boys and girls of a church, because a mission Bible School is designed for children in a community which has no church. Sunday School workers who are genuinely concerned about all boys and girls will take advantage of opportunities they have to serve in a mission Vacation Bible School.

Special materials have been prepared for use in such schools. These materials are graded for younger children (grades 1–3) and older children (grades 4–6). Like other Vacation Bible School materials, the mission series materials are available from Baptist Book Stores. These materials contain guidance for five three-hour sessions and are designed to benefit children who have little or no Bible background and church experience.

Other than to teach in a mission school, what can a Sunday School worker do to encourage his church to provide one or more mission Bible schools? He can lend enthusiastic support when his church considers promoting a mission School. He can encourage others to serve in the School. He can help the faculty prepare for its work. And he can pray diligently for the success of the mission Bible School.

3. *Backyard Bible Club*

The newest type of Vacation Bible School adventure is Backyard Bible Club. Materials for Backyard Bible Clubs are planned for elementary-age children. Two major items are provided: a teacher's book, called a Tell-a-Story, and Scripture Cards for the boys and girls to take home.

The daily schedule of approximately one and a half hours includes a Bible story with a follow-up Bible activity, a present-day story, games, songs, refreshments, and prayer. The teaching materials contain suggestions for five club meetings. These meetings may be held on successive days, the most common arrangement, or they may be held over a longer period of time.

A Backyard Bible Club may be held anywhere that a group

of boys and girls may be gathered—in a backyard as the name suggests, in a basement or garage, on a patio. The time of day best suited to the children can be used as the meeting time. A club needs a hostess who provides the meeting place and prepares and serves the refreshments, a teacher who guides the meetings and tells the stories, and several assistant teachers to help with large- and small-group work.

The simplicity of the program makes it possible for almost anyone to sponsor and conduct a Backyard Bible Club. Many teachers of boys and girls in Sunday School will want to have one or more Backyard Bible Clubs in their homes. If not, workers may still encourage their churches to sponsor clubs throughout the community.

4. *Weekday Bible Study*

Weekday Bible Study is a church-sponsored program of Bible study designed to complement what is being done through the other educational programs of the church. It is an ongoing age-graded Bible course with emphasis on gaining knowledge of Bible content. As a rule a Weekday Bible Study class meets for thirty sessions, each approximately one hour in length. Specially designed courses are available for fourth, fifth, and sixth graders, and for junior and senior high students.

Weekday Bible Study offers a solid opportunity to meet the need for more study of the Bible. It utilizes time between Sundays which might otherwise be lost to Bible study. It rounds out a child's Bible experiences, giving him a plus which cannot be gained from purely secular education.

If these paragraphs have stimulated your interest in Weekday Bible Study, you may wish to share your interest with the director of your Sunday School or with the extension director of the Sunday School. Further information may be gained by examining the leaflet *Weekday Bible Study* available from your state Sunday School office. Should such a program be started in your church, you can further help by encouraging boys and girls to participate. From time to time you can check on their progress and assure them of your continuing interest in their study.

VI. SUMMARY AND REVIEW

Let's think for just a minute about the ultimate purpose of all these things we have been discussing. Briefly stated, that purpose is to live out the Christian message so that pupils, prospects, and parents understand the depth of Christ's love and the reality of the workers' concern for them. With this purpose in mind, consider the following paragraphs.

1. The chapter talks about the purposes for which a worker should visit in a home. For which of these purposes have you visited with members, prospects, and their families in the past six months? For which purposes do you presently need to visit?

2. List the ministry needs of families, pupils, and prospects assigned to you. Are there some actions which you should take immediately?

3. The chapter also talked about Bible study opportunities other than Sunday School. Which of these opportunities does your church provide? What can you personally do to help the children you teach become involved in additional Bible study opportunities?

4. Pray that God will help you convey his love through your weekday contact with boys and girls and their parents.

Chapter 6
Providing Space, Equipment, and Furnishings for Teaching

The rooms in which we teach are silent partners in the teaching-learning process. Their influence upon what takes place within them is enormous. As silent partners in the enterprise, they can make learning a much happier and more effective process. Or rooms can handicap both teacher and learner. But either way, there is no way to escape the fact that our rooms are our partners.

This chapter will help you determine whether or not the room in which you teach is a good partner, an indifferent partner, or a poor one. The chapter should also give you some ideas for helping your department room make a greater contribution to the good teaching which you seek to do.

I. PROVIDING ADEQUATE SPACE FOR A CHILDREN'S DEPARTMENT

It is easy to say that a department room for children in grades one through six should contain a minimum of so many square feet, that a certain type of floor covering is best, and that chairs and tables should meet certain specifications. To make this discussion more meaningful for you, however, let's approach the topic from three directions. First, let's talk about what is best to provide if you are building new space. Second, although the same principles apply, let's talk about what you may do to adapt an older building. And third, let's deal with special space problems which may be troubling you. You will want to read all three sections, regardless of your particular situation.

1. *If You Are Building*

Department rooms without classrooms are recommended for all Children's departments. This does not mean that all children from grade one through grade six are taught in exactly the same way. A department room is merely a physical facility; it affects, but does not absolutely determine, the teaching approaches which are used in it.

Department rooms are recommended for a number of reasons. Let's take a look at the major reasons.

- Working in small groups within a classroom is a standard procedure in most public schools. Therefore, children are accustomed to working in such settings. They are not unduly distracted by activities taking place in other parts of the room.

- A large open space has a good psychological effect upon learners. As a rule, they feel more freedom to try new ideas. In contrast, small walled or curtained space tends to encourage teachers to use methods which require children to sit and listen.

- A department room without classrooms gives the department director needed opportunities to be fully aware of what is taking place in each small group. Such knowledge is hard to come by when small groups are shut away behind closed doors.

- The department director can easily be drawn into a small group to act as a resource person or to help the teacher handle problems with which the teacher wants his assistance.

- A department room allows greater flexibility in grouping

pupils for special purposes. If desirable, for instance, two small groups may be temporarily put together for some common activity such as viewing a filmstrip or talking with a resource person.

- The shift from small groups to the large group is usually handled with less wasted time and motion. If space is limited, children can remain at their small-group tables. Merely by turning their chairs the children can better see the department director.

- In such a setting, department resources are easily accessible to everyone. A minimum of time is needed to take materials from the supply shelves to any small group and to return unused materials at the end of the session.

- Churches which build department rooms without classrooms generally save construction and maintenance dollars.

Granted that a department room without classrooms is the best type of space for a Children's department, the next question is: How much space does a Children's department need?

The rule of thumb is twenty-five square feet of floor space for each person enrolled. Since the recommended maximum enrollment for a Children's department is thirty, the largest room needed is 25 feet wide by 30 feet long.

Applying the rule of thumb to a small enrollment would indicate that only 250 square feet would be needed for a department of ten, including workers and pupils. But be careful: furnishings and equipment require virtually the same amount of space even though enrollment is far below the recommended maximum. And note this limitation: such a small room would allow no room for growth.

So what minimum size should be considered when a church provides new space? In view of all the factors involved, no Children's department room should be less than 20 feet wide by 30 feet long.

As you have noticed, the suggested dimensions indicate rectangular rooms. The same amount of floor space can be achieved in a square room, a triangular room, or a circular room. The rectangle is the best shape, however.

Obviously, there is more to desirable space than more size and shape. The following listing should be given serious consideration by a church planning a new building or considering the rearranging of departments in present buildings.

Accessibility.—A Children's department room should open directly into a main hallway, preferably near an outside entrance.

Toilet facilities.—Rooms for younger children should have adjoining rest rooms. In some situations a rest room may be located between two departments. No Children's department should be far from a rest room, not even a department for older children.

Sink.—If possible, provide a sink for use with art and other activities.

Drinking fountains.—If possible, fountains of proper height should be located in hallways near all Children's department rooms.

Windows.—Clear glass is preferred for obvious reasons. Sills should be low enough that children can easily see out. Younger children particularly benefit from such provision.

Floors.—Use a covering that is resilient, noise resistant, and easily maintained. Good grades of commercial carpeting may be practical even though such carpeting is initially expensive.

Ceilings.—Acoustical tile or acoustical board is preferred.

Walls.—Walls should be stationary, as soundproof as practical, and should be painted with washable paint.

If your church is making plans for future building or rearrangement of your space, contact your state's church architecture department or the Church Architecture Department of The Sunday School Board of the Southern Baptist Convention, 127 Ninth Avenue, North, Nashville, Tennessee 37234, for help.

2. *If You Are Using Older Space*

Perhaps your department must use an assembly room and classrooms. If possible, consider remodeling the space to meet as closely as possible the standards you would set for space in a new building.

But suppose that remodeling is out of the question? There are good reasons why a church may not be able to do the extensive remodeling which would be involved.

First, the walls which separate classrooms from one another or from an assembly room may be weight-bearing walls. Removing them is simply not possible.

Second, a church may already be engaged in a building program which gives a low priority to remodeling space presently occupied by Children's departments.

Third, finances may indicate that remodeling at the present time is impossible or simply unwise.

Curriculum materials for use in all Children's departments are prepared with the realization that many departments must use less than ideal space. But there are several simple steps which can be taken to make an arrangement of classrooms and assembly room more effective. For instance, if a table large enough for good work overcrowds a small classroom, pupils may work with lapboards. While lapboards may be purchased, simple ones may also be made from sturdy cardboard.

In some buildings small classrooms are separated by folding walls. In such an instance, the wall may be opened. The combined space can then be used by one group while the other group uses an area in the assembly room.

Another step which many departments have taken to make old space more usable is to remove classroom doors. This permits the department director to be more easily involved in and aware of small-group work. It also helps to create the feeling of openness which generally has a good effect upon pupils.

Compare your present department space to the suggestions made under "If You Are Building." List the steps which you may realistically hope to take to bring your space closer to the ideal. Then in cooperation with necessary individuals and committees in your church, schedule the taking of these steps as soon as possible. For instance, painting is often a good first step.

3. *If You Have Special Space Problems*

In the previous section of the chapter, we talked mainly about adapting an arrangement of assembly room and classrooms. The assumption was that the total available space was adequte for a Children's department. But you may face the problem of too little space no matter how much remodeling you do. Is there any way to make a too small room more usable? Here are some ideas for you to consider.

● Remove the large but seldom used pieces of furnishings. Later in this chapter we will talk about some substitutions which might be made for these pieces.

● Get rid of all tables and chairs you do not need. Many departments are crowded because the workers feel that they must have two sets of chairs, one for small-group work and one for the large group. Chairs used for the small groups may also be used for the large group. In fact, large groups may be conducted with children still seated at their tables.

● Create a feeling of greater space by removing pictures and other objects which give a cluttered look to the room. These items, if worth using, may be stored and then used later as there is real reason to do so.

● Store or discard completed projects once they have been shared with the large group.

● Take steps to control noise. Even though you cannot see or touch noise, noise still can make a room seem smaller. If acoustical tile or acoustical board for the ceiling is out of the question, consider the possibility of carpet and curtains.

● Check your room arrangement to be sure floor space is used to best advantage. Later in the chapter we will talk about room arrangements. Examine that section for ideas on how best to use whatever floor space is available to you.

It is possible that your space problem is less common than the problems which have been discussed in this section. Maybe your department is also used as a corridor for some groups to get to their department rooms. Maybe the classrooms your department must use do not adjoin the space available for large group. There is not space in this book to deal with every space problem which may arise. The most important thing to remember in seeking solutions to space problems is that you are seeking to provide good Bible-learning experiences for boys and girls. Ask yourself (and your fellow workers): What is the best way we can use this space, even if usual procedures must be altered, to help boys and girls gain real Bible knowledge and insight? Then do not feel that the solution you achieve is impossible just because "it isn't in the book."

II. EQUIPPING AND FURNISHING A DEPARTMENT ROOM

As important as is the amount of space available for a Children's department, how that room is furnished and equipped is equally important. It is not enough simply to provide a department room with twenty-five square feet of floor space per child, beautifully painted and carpeted and with acoustical tile for a ceiling. For the most effective teaching, that bare room needs some furnishings and equipment. Let's look now at these needs.

Remember, there is only one reason for having any piece of furniture or equipment. Each item should contribute to the effectiveness of the learning process. Some items do so by creating physical comfort which releases energy for learning. Some items provide the means to tease young minds into learning. Some items simply make materials easily available.

1. *If You Can Have Everything*
- Chairs.—A height of 12 inches is suitable for most first and second graders; 14 inches is right for third and fourth graders; and 16 inches is best for fifth and sixth graders. Whatever chair height is provided, it is generally best to have all chairs the same height in a room.
- Tables for small-group activities.—Rectangular tables at least 30 by 48 inches in size and 10 inches higher than the seats of the chairs in use in the room are recommended. One table is needed for about every six to eight chairs, though not all the chairs need to be placed at the tables. Be careful that tables do not fill all the available space.

- Open shelves.—Open shelves are needed for work materials such as art supplies and nature materials. These units should be movable. Each unit should be about 14 to 16 inches deep, 42 to 46 inches high, with shelves 12 to 14 inches apart with a closed back. Each unit should be about 3 to 4 feet in length and should have a solid base.
- Bookrack.—Slanting shelves, placed about 12 to 14 inches apart, are preferred.
- Record player.—The record player should have three or four speeds and good tone quality.
- Cabinet for recordings.
- Piano.—A studio-size upright piano with a good tone is most desirable.
- ChronAharP or Autoharp.—Either of these instruments has a wide variety of uses and provides a good substitute for a piano.
- Tackboard.—The board should be 24 to 30 inches in depth and from 6 to 12 feet in length, depending upon the wall space available. The tackboard should be placed approximately 30 inches from the floor.
- Chalkboard.—The size of the chalkboard is determined by available space. Many workers in departments for older children find uses for a portable board.
- Picture rail.—The rail should be placed on the front wall, approximately 30 inches from the floor. If sufficient wall space is available, the rail should be at least 12 feet long.
- Supply cabinet.—A wall-hung cabinet or a storage closet is essential. The cabinet or closet should accommodate large items such as poster board and newsprint (24 by 36 inches).
- Paint rack.—This item is useful in departments for children through fourth grade.
- Picture file desk.
- Sink.—This optional item should be equipped with a mixing faucet, and adjoining counter tops should be Formica or a similar material.

● Portable coatrack for children's wraps.
● Shades or curtains.—Provision for protection from glare and for darkening the room for projected visuals is highly desirable.
● Access to a screen and projectors (film and filmstrip).
● Wastebasket

2. *If You Cannot Have Everything*

Few of us ever have the privilege of teaching in a room with perfect equipment and furnishings. We can dream about such a situation, but in reality we have to make many compromises. Let's consider solutions for some of the common problems which Children's workers face in the area of furnishings and equipment.

(1) *When You Lack Some Items*

Chairs and tables are two items which are essential. However, if the recommended tables are not possible, sturdy folding tables or lapboards can serve as substitutes.

If you do not have a good piano, someone in the department can learn to play the Autoharp or ChromAharP. Not all music can be played on these instruments, but many songs can. Even if you do not purchase one of these instruments for your department, you may be able to borrow one or to share one with another department.

A record player can serve some of the same purposes as a piano. Playing a record can set a mood, serve as a signal, or provide accompaniment for singing. Though you may not be able to purchase a record player for your department, you may be able to borrow a portable one for Sunday use. Some portables even operate on flashlight batteries.

Open shelves and the bookrack serve the important purpose of making resource materials easily available for everyone in the room. If it is not possible to provide these items, materials and books can be placed on chairs, a table, or on windowsills. If this arrangement must be made, be prepared to store all items between sessions.

Or it may be possible to substitute less desirable shelves. The important thing is that the shelves be deep enough to store materials conveniently. Even bricks and planks can be stacked to make a successful substitute.

Any substitute for the tackboard must enable workers to attach necessary materials to a wall surface. At the same time the substitute item should leave the wall surface unharmed. With most substitutes, special care must be taken to be sure that paints, felt-tip markers, and other media do not work through to mark the wall.

If no picture rail is available, pictures may be attached to the wall in a different way. Freezer-tape loops and Plasti-Tak are commonly used.

One of the hardest items for which to find a substitute is the wall supply cabinet or closet. However, many departments meeting in temporary quarters—in a public school, for instance—have solved their problem by using a number of cardboard boxes. Sometimes space storage through the week is available at some other place in the church building, though this arrangement may be inconvenient.

The picture file desk serves a dual purpose, providing a work surface for record taking and other activities as well as a place for storing pictures. A small table may be used for record taking, and pictures may be stored in cardboard or wooden boxes.

As was pointed out in the earlier listing, the chalkboard need not be permanently installed. Nor does it have to be large. If no chalkboard is available, newsprint or large sheets of wrapping paper can frequently serve as satisfactory substitutes.

(2) *When You Lack Money to Buy Furnishings and Equipment*

When money is a problem, consider having some items built locally. If someone in the church is willing to donate his time, you may be able to get the items at a great saving. The diagrams will be helpful if you decide to have your furniture manufactured locally.

It is also wise to develop a master plan for acquiring the items you need. List the items in the order of when you would like to acquire them. Over a period of time you may be able to obtain every item you desire.

(3) *When What You Have Is Inadequate*

Maybe your department is stuck with a piano with a terrible tone, donated by someone who really meant well. Or maybe your room is filled with makeshift equipment and furnishing. Either way, you have a challenge.

What does your own imagination tell you about getting rid of or improving the usability of the items you have? Could a table be made more useful by sawing a few inches off its legs? Could a cabinet with doors be made more useful by removing the doors? Could you swap one piece of unusable equipment for a piece of usable equipment; what you cannot use, someone else may be able to use.

3. *Diagrams for Making Furnishings and Equipment*

See pages 139 and 140 for drawings of possible room arrangement. Plans for constructing various items are also given.

III. ARRANGING A ROOM

This section of the chapter is designed to help you decide the best way to arrange your department room. The diagrams (not drawn to scale) represent ideal rooms with ideal furnishings and equipment. This means that departments with less than ideal furnishings and equipment should feel free to adapt the arrangements in the diagrams. Keep the following principles in mind.

- The purpose of room arrangement is improved teaching-learning. A good room arrangement makes materials easily accessible.
- A good arrangement says, Come in. It makes movement from the doorway to each small group easy.
- A good arrangement takes into account such factors as lighting and air flow.
- A good arrangement provides equally well for the small groups and for the large group.

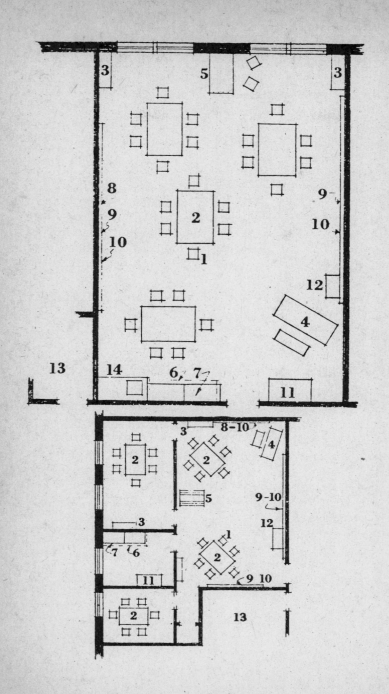

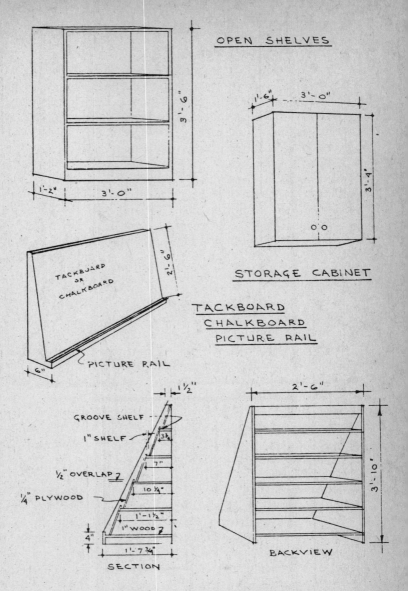

OPEN SHELVES

3'-6"

1'-2" 3'-0"

STORAGE CABINET

1'-6" 3'-0"

3'-4"

o o

TACKBOARD
OR
CHALKBOARD

2'-6"

6" PICTURE RAIL

TACKBOARD
CHALKBOARD
PICTURE RAIL

1½"

GROOVE SHELF

1" SHELF   3¾

7"

½" OVERLAP

10¼"

¼" PLYWOOD

1'-1½"

1" WOOD

4"

1'-7¾"

SECTION

2'-6"

3'-10"

BACKVIEW

BOOKRACK AND SHELVES

IV. PROVIDING SUPPLIES

As you use Southern Baptist curriculum materials prepared for Children's departments, you will find detailed listing of supplies needed for the teaching of each unit. This section merely lists basic supplies. Some of the items are actually categories of supplies while others refer to specific supplies.

- Literature.—In earlier chapters, the pieces of curriculum material available for and needed by each Children's department were described.
- Resource books for workers.—Three books comprise the basic set of books needed by workers in Children's departments. This book is one of them. The other two are *Guiding Children,* Rives and Sharp, and *Understanding Children,* Stith.
- Resource books for children.—Teachers' curriculum materials list with each unit some books which will be helpful for children to use.
- Hymnals.—Only older children actually use hymnals for singing in the department. However, workers in all Children's departments need supplementary music books. These books are listed in unit resources in the teachers' periodicals.
- Bibles.—Each department needs at least one Bible. Department Bible 1450BP is recommended because of its large type and pictures. From about the third grade on, children need access to several modern speech translations of the Bible. The *Broadman Presentation Bible* offers a wealth of resources in its supplementary section.
- Recordings.—Several good albums especially made for children are available. Each unit in the teachers' periodicals lists albums of particular value for use with the unit.
- Nature materials.—Nature materials are more frequently used in departments for younger children. They are, as a rule, seasonal. Tools for use in nature study include a magnifying glass, an aquarium, and a terrarium, flowerpots and planters, jars, and boxes for collections.

- Art supplies.—These materials include such items as crayons, paste, scissors, pencils, rulers, felt-tip pens, all kinds of paper for drawings and mountings, modeling clay, tempera paint, brushes, cellophane tape, masking tape, thumbtacks, pins, paper clips, aprons for painting and clay work, sentence strip paper and boards (a large board for large group activities and small boards for small group activities). Specific suggestions are given in the various periodicals.
- Drama activity supplies.—These materials include things such as scarves, pieces of cheesecloth, and simple costumes. Most materials needed for preparing simple settings and props are listed with art supplies.
- Maps.—Departments for older children use maps more frequently than do other Children's departments, although maps begin to be used with some regularity about the time children are in the third grade. Maps related to specific units of study are listed in the teachers' periodicals.

V. SUMMARY AND REVIEW

Consider the following questions, turning back through the chapter as you need to.

1. Which section of the chapter gave you the most ideas for improving the physical setting in which you teach?

2. What can you do toward solving problems related to
   - the amount of space provided for your department?
   - the quality of that space?
   - the furnishings and equipment available to your department?
   - the arrangement of the furnishings and equipment in your department room?
   - supplies for good teaching?

Chapter 7
Bus Outreach and Children's Worship

The big white bus glided to a stop at the sidewalk's edge. A grinning teen-ager swung down to stand beside the door as boys and girls single-filed off the bus and into the church building. The teen-ager spoke to each child and made sure that each child knew his bus number: seven.

At the close of the morning service, that same bus was once again at the curb. The same teen-ager and the same driver watched as boys and girls streamed from the auditorium to reboard the bus. In a few minutes, the bus moved into the after-church traffic and began to run its weekly route, once more delivering boys and girls to their homes.

One of the most interesting phenomenon in contemporary church life has been the upsurge in use of buses to reach into the communities surrounding our churches. Many a church which once struggled along with a low Sunday School attendance now confronts the exciting problem of too many people for too little space. Most of the persons being reached by bus outreach are boys and girls of elementary age.

Perhaps your church has purchased or rented one or more buses and is now running routes to pick up boys and girls each week. If so, this chapter offers some suggestions about ways to provide for bus children in Sunday School.

Or perhaps your church is just considering whether or not it should begin bus outreach. If this is the case, church leaders will find help by using *How to Build a Bus Ministry* by James E. Coggin and Bernard M. Spooner. This book gives complete step-by-step details for churches who are expanding or starting a bus ministry. *Outreach Through Bus Ministry* is a filmstrip which pictures an actual church performing its bus ministry. A bus captain takes us along with him so we can see firsthand the way this ministry works. (Fifty-two frames, color, manual, recording.)

I. PROVIDING FOR BUS CHILDREN IN SUNDAY SCHOOL

Bringing children to the church for Sunday School is not an end in itself, regardless of the method by which they are brought. A church which uses buses to reach the children in its community owes those children sound Bible-learning experiences after they arrive on Sunday morning. Different churches have met this challenge in different ways. This section of the chapter looks at some approaches to providing for bus children in Sunday School.

1. *In Regular Departments*

Regular Sunday School departments usually offer the best provision for bus children as long as the number of boys and girls being brought on the bus (or buses) is not too large. If the number is relatively small, they can be absorbed without too great difficulty. For instance, a church which has six Children's departments each with an enrollment of approximately twenty or so should be able to care for five or so additional boys and girls in each department without putting undue strain on organization or facilities. As long as the number of new children to be accommodated does not force the enrollment of any department over twenty-five or thirty, bus children can usually become a part of the departments which already exist.

In some churches the number of bus children may create a need for additional departments. This does not automatically mean that the new departments must be exclusively for children who ride the buses. It may only mean that more departments are needed and that each department will be composed both of children who ride the buses and of children who come to Sunday School by other means. In the organization and equipping of these new departments, the same principles apply as in the creation of any new department.

2. *Special Departments for Bus Children*

In some situations special departments for bus children are needed. This is usually the case if the number of children coming by bus is large in proportion to the number of children already attending the Sunday School. In such cases, it may not be feasible to absorb the bus children into already existing departments.

But why not simply create additional departments combining children who are bused and other children? One of the major reasons is that the bused children frequently are unfamiliar with church life. They may be unaccustomed to the routines of the usual Sunday School. They may not know basic Bible stories and teachings. If they come from a cultural background which differs from that of the children already attending the church, behavior problems which are difficult to handle in mixed groups are likely. The wiser course seems to be to provide special departments just for bus children.

These special departments may be set up on a temporary basis. Special curriculum materials are available for temporary departments. These materials are designed to help a child build basic Bible background and to be ready to participate profitably in the learning experiences provided through the regular curriculum. These materials are available from Materials Services Department, 127 Ninth Avenue, North, Nashville, Tennessee 37234,

These special materials include *Learning About the Bible, Teacher's Book*. This book contains guidance for thirteen sessions for children from grades one through six. It is designed for boys and girls who have little or no Bible background and little or no church experience. Each teacher in a temporary department should have a personal copy of this book.

The materials also include *Learning About the Bible, Pupil's Book.* This book contains favorite Bible stories, has Bible verses to learn, and carries other Bible-related activities. Each child in a temporary department should have a copy of his own.

An associated item is *Children's Worship,* a book offering guidance about handling worship experiences for children reached through a bus program. Later in this chapter we will talk more about this matter.

Departments for children brought to the church by bus may also be permanent. Let's take a look at some reasons why a church might decide to have permanent departments:

● The number of bused children may be too large for absorption into already existing departments due to problems of space, equipment, or personnel.

● The bused children's deficiencies in Bible knowledge and skills may be so great as to indicate the need for continuing separate provision.

● Bused children may be brought to the church at a time other than the regular Sunday School hour. Such a situation could even exist on Sunday morning with bus departments provided during the regular worship service hour, for instance.

(1) *Bus Departments Are Departments*

If you were to ask, "How does a bus department differ from any other Sunday School department for children?" the answer could be stated simply. Basically the only difference is in the children enrolled in the department. All of the basic principles of organization, staffing, and provision which have been described in this book pertain equally to departments for children who are bused. These departments need the same teacher-pupil ratios, the same enrollment limits, the same square footage per member, and the same equipment.

There is one point at which a distinction may be made. This point is the matter of curriculum materials. A department designed specifically for bused children may use the bus outreach curriculum materials described earlier in this chapter when it is first organized and then move into the use of the Foundation Series. These materials are described in the special sections on Bible Learners, Bible Discoverers, and Bible Searchers.

(2) *Special Problems of Bus Departments*

Many departments in churches which are busing children, particularly if large numbers are involved, do face some special problems. This section of the chapter is intended to offer a few tips for handling some of the major problems which are most frequently confronted.

One common problem is large enrollments which make using the procedures and schedules suggested in curriculum materials hard to handle. To solve this problem, the time available for Sunday School may arbitrarily be divided into halves: half for small-group work and half for large-group time. Boys and girls may be permanently assigned to small groups, and teachers may provide Bible-learning activities which can be completed within one session. Such activities may be taken from the puzzles, Bible games, and introductory activities given in the teacher's material and in the corresponding pupil's book.

Another idea which has found acceptability in some Sunday Schools is to divide those present into two equal groups. While one section works in small groups, the other section is involved in a large-group learning experience. When the session is half over, the situation is reversed.

Limited space sometimes prevents a department from doing well those projects which require a lot of space. In such situations, the major emphasis may be placed on large-group activities. By using suggestions for games and puzzles, individual participation may be built into these large-group experiences. If space permits, the large-group time could be followed by small-group work in which discussion, games, and other activities suited to a limited space are workable. Or in some such situations small-group work is possible if workers are careful to select projects which require only limited space.

Inexperienced teachers sometimes have difficulty in guiding boys and girls in the best learning experiences. Of course, the starting point in solving this problem is to seek out teachers who are willing to study and to plan in order to improve as teachers. A beginning point could be group study of *Guiding Children,* Rives and Sharp. As a help for inexperienced teachers, select the curriculum pieces that best fit the level of the boys and girls.

Irregularity of attendance among bused children sometimes presents a problem. Workers find it difficult to use projects which extend over a period of weeks. One solution to this problem is to accent learning activities which require only one Sunday to complete. Sometimes a project which extends over several Sundays can be broken into parts, each requiring only one Sunday. For instance, a small group may have as its project to pantomime stories from the unit. Each Sunday one story can be reviewed, and the pantomiming for that story can be planned and carried out within the session.

II. CONDUCTING CHILDREN'S WORSHIP

In recent years more and more churches have been asking a significant question: Just what is the best provision to make for worship experiences for boys and girls? Some churches have reached the conclusion that adult-oriented worship services need to be amended to better meet the needs of children. Others have decided that the best way to meet the needs of the boys and girls and of the adult worshipers in the congregation is to provide a separate worship service altogether. Separate provision seems to be especially popular with churches which bus large numbers of children to Sunday School. However, many of these churches have introduced special features into the regular worship service. Perhaps the pastor invites the children in the congregation to join him at the front of the auditorium early in the service as he tells them a story of particular interest.

Just what has lead churches to consider changing their traditional patterns? Actually a number of factors have been operating.

These include overcrowding in regular worship services. Growing churches are often confronted with having to devise some way to provide for worshipers in limited space. One solution has been to conduct a worship service for children while adults and youth are in Sunday School and then to conduct a similar service for adults and youth while children are in Sunday School.

Another reason churches have considered separate provision for children in worship has sometimes been the presence of large numbers of unattended children in the regular worship services. This situation may easily occur in churches which are busing large numbers of children. It may also occur in communities with many children of elementary-school age. These unattended children can create problems in the congregation. Frequently, they have little church experience and really do not understand what is expected of them in worship. Even if they have a fair understanding of what is expected of them, they may be too immature to conduct themselves properly without adequate supervision. Some churches have tried to solve this problem by providing church parents for children whose families do not come to the worship services. That is, Mr. and Mrs. Brown agree to have Tim Jones, Bill Haver, and Sammy Mason sit with them each Sunday morning. The Browns either call for the boys at their departments or establish some agreed-upon meeting place. If the boys come by bus, the Browns make sure that each boy for whom they are responsible in the worship services gets to his correct bus immediately following the worship service.

Some churches have given serious consideration to separate provision because they have become aware that boys and girls of elementary-school age are not deeply involved in the worship experiences offered in the regular services. Sometimes this awareness has come because the children create disturbances in the regular services. In such situations the best solution may not be separate provision so much as the introduction of special elements into the regular services. These elements may include the use of a special time for the pastor and children. Songs familiar to children may also be used for congregational singing.

But this section of Chapter 7 is designed to help those churches who have come to the conclusion that a separate service for children is the best solution in their situation.

1. *What Is Children's Worship?*

In this chapter the term "Children's Worship" refers to a special worship service for boys and girls of elementary-school age. It is assumed that this service is conducted on the children's level of understanding and that it provides adequate opportunities for their active participation. Sometimes this service is called "Children's Church." However, the children who participate are not actually a church.

Children's Worship may be provided for all children who attend without their parents. Or it may be provided only for bused children. Or it may be provided for all children even though their parents do attend the regular worship services.

The purpose of Children's Worship is to provide more meaningful worship experiences for the boys and girls than is possible in the framework of the regular worship services. This statement is, or ought to be, true even if a church begins Children's Worship merely as a way of dividing the congregation in order to meet a space problem or merely because the children are creating a disturbance in the regular worship services.

Just because a church initiates Children's Worship, it need not continue the practice from that day forward. In some churches Children's Worship may be a temporary measure. For instance, the church which sets up Children's Worship primarily because of a space problem may terminate the arrangement as soon as it can provide space adequate for the entire church family to worship together. Or a church may temporarily operate Children's Worship in order to help a group of bused children develop an adequate understanding and appreciation for worship. When church leaders feel that the children have developed the necessary appreciations and skills to participate meaningfully with other members of the congregation in the regular worship service, Children's Worship may be discontinued.

2. *Organizing for Children's Worship*

If a church feels that it should begin Children's Worship, just what steps are necessary in order to get started? This section will attempt to answer this basic question.

(1) *Determine How Many Worship Services to Provide*

For best results, it is advisable to keep groups of children limited to about thirty for purposes of worship as well as for educational purposes. This means that a church should plan one service for each thirty children for whom it proposes to provide Children's Worship. If there are from thirty to sixty children, two services will be required. Sixty to ninety children would require three worship services, and so on.

If more than one worship service is to be provided for children in grades one through six, the division can be done on the basis of grades. Two services may be set up with one service for first through third graders and the other for fourth through sixth graders. Three services would allow a two-grade span in each grouping.

(2) *Secure Capable Leaders*

Each group should have a worship leader and at least three associates. The titles given to these persons may vary from church to church. The leader should of course be a person who understands children, loves them, and is willing to work diligently to provide them the best of experiences. His associates should be just as dedicated, though they may well be youth with considerably less experience with children than the leader has. At least two of the associates should be musicians. One can serve as the pianist or organist. And the other can serve as the song leader. Many churches follow a plan of rotating associate leaders so that youth who serve in these positions are not permanently deprived of the enrichment which comes from participation in the regular worship services of the church.

These factors should be considered in seeking persons to lead in Children's Worship, whether as leaders or associates:

● Each person sought should be a Christian who is growing in his Christian experience.

● Each person should see the potential which children have

for spiritual growth and should have the understanding and patience required to guide that growth.

● Each of these persons should be dependable and should be willing to make careful preparation for carrying out his assignments.

● Each person sought as a leader for Children's Worship should hold a sound biblical view of conversion. During elementary school years many, many children confront the demands of Christ upon those who would become his followers. A faulty understanding of conversion can cause a leader to make serious errors in guiding children in this crucial decision.

(3) *Train Workers for Children's Worship*

Those who would be good worship leaders must grow in their understanding of children. Worship leaders should review the basic books designed to help workers know how to teach children. These books include:

Understanding Children by Marjorie Stith
Guiding Children by Elsie Rives and Margaret Sharp
Other books which these workers will find quite helpful are:
When Can a Child Believe? by Eugene Chamberlain
Children and Conversion, edited by Clifford Ingle
New Dimensions in Teaching Children by Robert G. Fulbright.

Additional help in understanding their task may be found in *Children's Worship* and *Children's Worship Service Helps,* both prepared in the Children's Section; Sunday School Department, of The Sunday School Board of the Southern Baptist Convention. *Children's Worship* is available from the Materials Services Department of The Sunday School Board, *Children's Worship Service Helps, released* by Convention Press, is available in Baptist Book Stores.

3. *Determining Ingredients for Children's Worship*

The format for Children's Worship will vary somewhat from situation to situation. Some of the basic ingredients will remain the same since the purpose is to provide good worship experiences. These basic ingredients are as follows.

(1) *Music*

Both instrumental quiet music and group singing are almost inevitably a part of Christian worship. Songs used should of course be those which have meaning for the children. This does not mean that every song must be a catchy chorus with which children are already familiar. It does mean that hymns with difficult melodies and difficult symbolism in their words are generally to be avoided.

(2) *Call to Worship*

In many services some sort of call to worship will be used. The call to worship need not necessarily be musical.

(3) *Use of the Bible*

It is difficult to imagine a regular worship service which does not use the Bible. Use of the Bible is even more important in Children's Worship. Their use should involve a wide variety of methods, requiring and encouraging active participation by the children rather than merely passive listening.

(4) *Offering*

Some church leaders may assume that, because the children for whom the worship service is being provided lack financial resources, no offering should be taken. To fail to provide children with this opportunity to respond to God is to shortchange them. As limited as may be their resources, children need the opportunity to give.

(5) *Prayer*

In Children's Worship prayer will take many forms. Silent prayers, sentence prayers, guided prayers, and traditionally lead prayers are all to be used as appropriate.

(6) *Bible Story or Sermon*

Perhaps one of the most crucial features in Children's Worship is that portion which corresponds to the sermon in the regular worship service. The leader will have opportunity to apply the Bible truths to child-life situations and to use illustrations within the children's understanding. Because of the short attention span of children, this feature will as a rule be quite different from the traditional sermon. Sometimes it will more closely resemble a simple Bible story. Sometimes the feature may resemble guided Bible story. It will usually allow room for some sort of group participation other than mere listening. Almost inevitably the feature of Bible emphasis will be shorter than the usual sermon of twenty-five to thirty minutes.

(7) *Response*

Worshipers in any service of a church need to be given opportunity to express their responses. This fact is one which requires honest recognition and thoughtful handling when the worshipers are children of elementary-school age. There will obviously be times when children need the opportunity to make professions of faith. Perhaps more often they will need opportunities to express their interest in beginning or continuing in the Christian life. If invitations are given in the traditional way, the worship leader should exercise care to ensure that each decision is valid. As a rule, children registering decisions in such circumstances require individual guidance.

(8) *Refreshments*

Because many children who are normally reached by buses may not have breakfast, some churches feel that bus children need some sort of refreshments if they are to remain at the church throughout the entire morning. This time is usually provided after Sunday School and before the worship service actually begins.

4. *Resources for Conducting Children's Worship*

Two resources for guiding Children's Worship have already been mentioned. *Children's Worship* provides thirteen outlines for worship services for children as well as general guidance for determining the circumstances under which such services should be initiated. *Children's Worship Service Helps* provides suggestions for fifty-two worship services. The introductory material in this book also offers general guidelines for establishing and maintaining Children's Worship.

In addition, *Children's Leadership*, the quarterly publication about which you have already read, provides guidance on a continuing basis. Each issue of the magazine contains thirteen dated outlines for Children's Worship services.

Besides providing these thirteen outlines for use by churches which are already providing weekly Children's Worship, this publication offers help to churches which are using other approaches to involving children in meaningful worship. Each issue carries some tips on ways to involve elementary-age children more adequately in the regular worship services.

III. SUMMARY AND REVIEW

A few thought questions can help you evaluate what you have gained through reading this chapter. You may wish to make notes.

● If your church is presently considering beginning bus outreach, what could you suggest that leaders read to help them in making that decision?

● If your church is presently busing children to Sunday School, how do you feel their needs can best be met, by including them in regular departments or by setting up special departments for them? Why?

● If church leaders asked your opinion concerning whether to begin separate worship services for boys and girls in grades one through six, how would you respond? What reasons could you give to support your view?

● If your church provides Children's Worship, what constructive suggestions can you make for improving these services?

Personal Learning Activities

Chapter 1

1. State briefly what you hope to accomplish by studying this book.
2. How would you answer if asked to explain why you consider teaching children in Sunday School to be important?

Chapter 2

1. How many departments are needed in the Children's Division in the Sunday School of your church?
2. Name at least seven characteristics of a good Children's Sunday School worker.
3. In light of the suggestions in the chapter, evaluate the way in which you were enlisted as a Children's Sunday School worker.
4. List your duties as a Sunday School worker.
5. What are the major steps a Children's Sunday School department must take in preparing for outreach?
6. How can your department improve in its use of records as a resource for better reaching and teaching boys and girls?
7. Name the three basic books which every worker with Children in Sunday School should study.

Chapter 3

1. Review the physical, intellectual, social, emotional, and spiritual characteristics of boys and girls in the grade(s) with which you work. Write a brief statement indicating the degree to which you have observed these characteristics in the children with whom you work.
2. List the basic curriculum pieces needed for use with and by

the children you teach. What leisure reading piece should be provided for your department?

3. How should the children whom you teach be grouped for teaching and reaching?
4. List two suggestions for helping the children you teach use the Bible.
5. List four or more ways to help the pupils you teach learn memory verses.

Chapter 4

1. What is the one single greatest weakness in the planning done by the department in which you work?
2. What immediate step could be taken to offset this weakness?
3. What tools have you found in this chapter which may be of use in your department's planning?
4. In light of the information concerning schedules, how wisely has your department been using its time?

Chapter 5

1. List the purposes for which you have visited with members, prospects, and their families in the past six months. For what purposes do you presently need to visit?
2. List the ministry needs of families, pupils, and prospects assigned to you. Place a star beside actions which you should take immediately.
3. What Bible study opportunities other than Sunday School does your church provide?
4. List at least two ways you can help the children you teach to become involved in additional Bible study opportunities.

Chapter 6

1. Following the suggestions in the chapter, prepare an appraisal of the space presently used by your department.

2. List the equipment, furnishings, and basic materials which your department lacks.
3. Prepare a sketch showing what you consider to be the best arrangement of furnishings now possible in your department.
4. Identify any space problem(s) your department has and briefly state a possible solution.

Chapter 7

1. If your church is presently considering beginning bus outreach, what resources could you suggest that leaders use to help them in making that decision?
2. If your church is presently busing children to Sunday School, how do you feel their needs can best be met, by including them in regular departments or by setting up special departments for them? Why?
3. If church leaders asked your opinion concerning whether to begin separate worship services for boys and girls in grades one through six, how would you respond? What reasons could you give to support your view?
4. If your church provides Children's Worship, what constructive suggestions can you make for improving these services?

The Church Study Course

The Church Study Course consists of a variety of short-term credit courses for adults and youth and non-credit foundational units for children and preschoolers. The materials are for use in addition to the study and training curriculums made available to the churches on an ongoing basis.

Study courses and foundational units are organized into a system that is promoted by the Sunday School Board, 127 Ninth Avenue, North, Nashville, Tennessee 37234, through the departments in the Church Services and Materials Division; by the Woman's Missionary Union, 600 North Twentieth Street, Birmingham, Alabama 35203; by the Brotherhood Commission, 1548 Poplar

Avenue, Memphis, Tennessee 38104; and the respective departments of the state conventions affiliated with the Southern Baptist Convention.

Study course materials are flexible enough to be adapted to the needs of any Baptist church. The resources are published in several different formats—textbooks of various sizes, workbooks, and kits. Each item contains a brief explanation of the Church Study Course and information on requesting credit. Additional information and interpretation are available from the participating agencies.

Types of Study and Credit

Adults and youth can earn study course credit through individual or group study. Youth may take adult courses for credit, but adults can receive credit for youth courses only by teaching them to youth. Teachers of courses or of foundational units are eligible to receive credit.

1. Class Experience.—Group involvement with course material for the designated number of hours for the particular course. A person who is absent from one or more sessions must complete the "Personal Learning Activities" or other requirements for the material missed.

2. Individual Study.—This includes reading, viewing, or listening to course material and completing the specified requirements for the course.

3. Lesson Course Study.—Parallel use of designated study course material during the study of selected units in Church Program Organization periodical curriculum units. Guidance for this means of credit appear in the selected periodical.

4. Institutional Study.—Parallel use of designated study course material during regular courses at educational institutions, including Seminary Extension Department courses. Guidance for this means of credit is provided by the teacher.

Credit is awarded for the successful completion of a course of study. This credit is granted by the Church Study Course Awards Office, 127 Ninth Avenue, North, Nashville, Tennessee 37234, for the participating agencies. Form 151 (available free) is recommended for use in requesting credit.

When credit is issued to a person on request, the Awards Office sends two copies of a notice of credit earned to the church. The original copy of the credit slip should be filed by the study course clerk in the participant's record of training folder. The duplicate should be given to the person who earned the credit. Accumulated credits are applied toward leadership or member development diplomas, which are measures of learning, growth, development, and training.

Detailed information about the Church Study Course system of credits, diplomas, and record keeping is available from the participating agencies. Study course materials, supplementary teaching or learning aids, and forms for record keeping may be ordered from Baptist Book Stores.

How to Request Credit for This Course

This book is the text for course 6314 of Subject Area 63, Sunday School Leadership.

This course is designed for seven and one-half (7½) hours of group study. Credit is awarded for satisfactory class experience with the study material for the minimum number of hours. If supervised practice or laboratory experience is appropriate and is used, two hours of such guided activity may be substituted for one hour of class time, provided that at least one half of the required hours is spent in classwork. A person who is absent for one or more sessions must complete the "Personal Learning Activities" or other requirements for the material missed.

Credit is also allowed for use of this material in individual study and institutional study, if so designated. Teachers of this course also are eligible to receive credit.

After the course is completed, the teacher, the study course clerk, or any person designated by the church should complete Form 151 ("Request for Course Credit") and send it to the Awards Office, 127 Ninth Avnue, North, Nashville, Tennessee 37234. Individuals also may request credit by writing the Awards Office.